Free Video Free Free Video

Essential Test Tips Video from Trivium Test Prep

Dear Customer,

Thank you for purchasing from Trivium Test Prep! We're honored to help you prepare for your GED exam.

To show our appreciation, we're offering a **FREE *GED Essential Test Tips* Video by Trivium Test Prep.*** Our video includes 35 test preparation strategies that will make you successful on the GED. All we ask is that you email us your feedback and describe your experience with our product. Amazing, awful, or just so-so: we want to hear what you have to say!

To receive your **FREE *GED Essential Test Tips* Video**, please email us at 5star@triviumtestprep.com. Include "Free 5 Star" in the subject line and the following information in your email:

1. The title of the product you purchased.
2. Your rating from 1 – 5 (with 5 being the best).
3. Your feedback about the product, including how our materials helped you meet your goals and ways in which we can improve our products.
4. Your full name and shipping address so we can send your **FREE *GED Essential Test Tips* Video**.

If you have any questions or concerns please feel free to contact us directly at 5star@triviumtestprep.com.

Thank you!

– Trivium Test Prep Team

*To get access to the free video please email us at 5star@triviumtestprep.com, and please follow the instructions above.

GED SCIENCE TEST PREP BOOK:
Study Guide and Practice Test Questions for the GED Exam

Jonathan Cox

Copyright © 2022 by Accepted, Inc.

ISBN-13: 9781637981979

ALL RIGHTS RESERVED. By purchase of this book, you have been licensed one copy for personal use only. No part of this work may be reproduced, redistributed, or used in any form or by any means without prior written permission of the publisher and copyright owner. Accepted, Inc.; Trivium Test Prep; Cirrus Test Prep; and Ascencia Test Prep are all imprints of Trivium Test Prep, LLC.

GED® Testing Service LLC was not involved in the creation or production of this product, is not in any way affiliated with Accepted, Inc., and does not sponsor or endorse this product. All test names (and their acronyms) are trademarks of their respective owners. This study guide is for general information only and does not claim endorsement by any third party.

Image(s) used under license from Shutterstock.com

Table of Contents

Introduction i

ONE: Scientific Practices 1
Scientific Inquiry 1
Designing Experiments 2
Facts, Theories, and Laws 3
Test Your Knowledge 5
Answer Key 7

TWO: Life Science 9
Biological Molecules 9
Nucleic Acids 11
Structure and Function of Cells 12
Cellular Respiration 14
Photosynthesis 15
Cell Division 16
Genetics 17
Evolution 19
Ecology 20
Human Anatomy and Physiology 22
Test Your Knowledge 30
Answer Key 33

THREE: Physical Science 37
The Structure of the Atom 37
The Periodic Table of the Elements 38
Chemical Bonds 40
Properties of Matter 42
States of Matter 43
Chemical Reactions 44
Mixtures 45
Acids and Bases 46
Motion 48
Forces 49
Work 50
Energy 50
Waves 52
Electricity and Magnetism 54
Test Your Knowledge 56
Answer Key 60

FOUR: Earth Science 65
Astronomy 65
Geology 67

Hydrology 68
Meteorology 70
Test Your Knowledge 72
Answer Key 74

FIVE: Practice Test 77
Answer Key 91

Introduction

Congratulations on choosing to take the GED exam! By purchasing this book, you've taken an important step on your path to earning your high school-equivalency credential.

This guide will provide you with a detailed overview of the GED exam so that you know exactly what to expect on test day. We'll take you through all the concepts covered on the exam and give you the opportunity to test your knowledge with practice questions. Even if it's been a while since you last took a major test, don't worry; we'll make sure you're more than ready!

What is the GED?

The General Educational Development, or GED, test is a high school-equivalency test—composed of four subtests—that certifies that the test-taker has high school-level academic skills. Forty states currently offer the GED test. The four subtests can be taken together or separately, but you must pass all four subtests in order to pass the test overall. Once a test-taker in one of those states passes the exam, then that person becomes eligible to receive a high school-equivalency diploma, which can be used in job applications or in applying to colleges or universities. The test is specifically designed for individuals who did not complete a high school diploma, no matter the reason.

What's on the GED?

The GED test gauges high school-level content knowledge and skills in four areas: Reasoning through Language Arts (RLA), Mathematical Reasoning, Science, and Social Studies. Candidates are expected to be able to read closely, write clearly, edit and understand standard written English as it is used in context, and solve quantitative and algebraic problems. You also must show strong content knowledge in life science, physical science, and Earth and space science as well as civics and government, United States history, geography and the world, and economics.

The test includes a variety of question types, including multiple-choice, drag-and-drop, hot spot, and fill-in-the-blank. The multiple-choice questions are a standard style in which the test-taker selects the best answer among a series of choices. In drag-and-drop questions, the test-taker must select the best answer, click on it, and drag it to the appropriate location. This usually involves sorting items into categories or making associations between different concepts. Hot spot questions require the test-taker to click on a specific area of an image. For fill-in-the-blank questions, the test-taker must type in the word or phrase missing from the statement or question. The Reasoning through Language Arts section also includes some questions in which the test-taker must select the best grammatical or punctuation change from a drop-down list of options as well as extended response questions that require the test-taker to type the answer.

Each subtest is taken separately. You must complete one subtest before moving on to the next. You will have 115 minutes for the math test, ninety minutes for the science test, seventy minutes for the social studies test, and 150 minutes for the Reasoning through Language Arts test.

What's on the GED Exam?

Skills Assessed	Topics	Percentage of Exam*
Reasoning Through Language Arts		
▶ Read closely	Informational texts	75%
▶ Write clearly		
▶ Edit and understand the use of standard written English in context	Literature texts	25%
Mathematical Reasoning		
▶ Understand key mathematical concepts	Quantitative problem-solving	45%
▶ Demonstrate skill and fluency with key math procedures		
▶ Apply concepts to realistic situations	Algebraic problem-solving	55%
Science		
▶ Use scientific reasoning (textually and quantitatively)	Life science	40%
	Physical science	40%
▶ Apply scientific reasoning to a variety of realistic situations	Earth and space science	20%

Skills Assessed	Topics	Percentage of Exam*
▶ Textual analysis ▶ Data representation ▶ Inference skills ▶ Problem-solving using social studies content	**Social Studies**	
	Civics and government	50%
	United States history	20%
	Economics	15%
	Geography and the world	15%

Percentages are approximate.

The Reasoning through Language Arts test assesses your ability to understand a range of texts which can be found in both academic and workplace settings. The test includes literary and informational texts as well as important US founding documents. The texts vary in length from 450 to 900 words. You will be asked to identify details and make logical inferences from—as well as valid claims about—the texts. You also will be asked to define key vocabulary and use textual evidence to analyze the texts in your own words in the form of a written response.

The Mathematical Reasoning test assesses mastery of key fundamental math concepts. Rather than focusing on specific content, the test focuses on reasoning skills and modes of thinking that can be used in a variety of mathematical content areas, specifically algebra, data analysis, and number sense. Questions will assess your ability to make sense of complex problems, use logical thinking to find solutions, recognize structure, and look for and express regularity in repeated reasoning. You also will be evaluated on the precision of your mathematics.

The Science test assesses your mastery of scientific content in life science, physical science, and Earth and space science, as well as your ability to apply scientific reasoning. Each question on the test will focus on one science practice and one content topic. Specifically, questions will relate to two primary themes: Human Health and Living Systems—all concepts related to the health and safety of all living things on the planet—and Energy and Related Systems—all concepts related to sources and uses of energy.

The Social Studies test assesses your mastery of both social studies content and skills. Each question addresses one element of social studies practice and one specific content topic. The primary focus of the test is on American civics and government, with the other three content areas as supplements. The questions address two core themes: Development of Modern Liberties and Democracy—which traces the current ideas of democracy from ancient times to present—and Dynamic Responses in Societal Systems, which addresses how society's systems, structures, and policies have developed and responded to each other.

Unique Question Types

While the majority of the GED exam is made up of multiple-choice questions, it also contains several other types of questions that might be unfamiliar to you. Collectively, these are called "technology-enhanced items" because they require you to interact with a computer. There are four types of these questions: drag-and-drop, hot spot, drop-down or cloze, and fill-in-the-blank. Each type of question is structured a little differently and requires different actions from the test-taker. Each type of question also assesses different skills. While they may seem a little intimidating, once you understand what these questions are testing and how to answer them, you will see they are quite manageable.

DRAG-and-DROP

A drag-and-drop question has three parts: the question or prompt, drop target, and tiles or "draggers." Each tile contains a small image, word, or numerical expression. You will read the question or prompt, and then click the tile you think has the correct answer, drag it to the target area, and then let it go. In some cases, you may be able to put more than one tile in a single target area, or you may be able to put the same tile in multiple target areas. If this is the case, a note included with the question will tell you that. For example, imagine a question says, *Classify the following fruits by color.* There is a response area for yellow, blue, green, and red, and tiles that say *apple*, *strawberry*, *blueberry*, *banana*, and *pear*. You would drag both the apple and strawberry tiles to the red target area. You would also put the apple tile in the green area.

Drag-and-drop questions will differ both in structure and in skills assessed, depending on the subtest. On the Mathematics subtest, drag-and-drop questions are primarily used for constructing expressions, equations, and inequalities. For example, the prompt will include a scenario and an incomplete equation. The tiles will contain various numerical and/or alphabetical variables and operators that could complete the equation. You must then drag the appropriate mathematical element to its spot in the equation. You also could be asked to order the steps in a mathematical process or solution or match items from two different sets.

On the Reasoning Through Language Arts (RLA) subtest, drag-and-drop questions will typically focus on sequencing and classifying to assess comprehension and analysis of a reading passage. Some questions may ask you to order events in a passage based on chronology or to illustrate cause and effect. Or you might be asked to classify evidence based on how it relates to the argument of a passage. Drag-and-drop questions on this subtest will usually incorporate graphic organizers, such as Venn diagrams, timelines, or charts.

On the Social Studies subtest, drag-and-drop questions are primarily used for mapping, classifying, and sequencing. For example, you might be asked to put the steps in a political process in the correct order, or you may be asked to sort actions based on the related constitutional freedom. Alternatively, you could be asked to place correct labels on the continents or use information from a brief text to place data points on a graph or chart.

On the Science subtest, drop-and-drag questions are used primarily for sequencing questions: placing the steps of a biological or chemical process in the correct order. These questions can also be used for classification, like sorting animals into mammals and non-mammals. Like on the RLA subtest, science drag-and-drop questions often utilize graphic organizers, like Venn diagrams.

EXAMPLE

1. The owner of a taco truck decides to use data to determine how many tacos he can make during a two-hour lunch rush. He has determined that the average time it takes to make five tacos is eight minutes.

   Complete the equation to show how the taco truck owner determined that he can make seventy-five tacos in two hours.

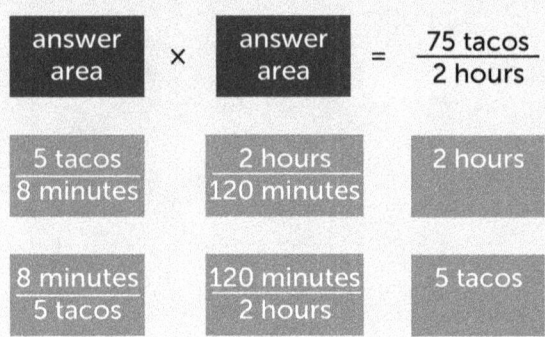

HOT SPOT

In a hot spot question, you will be presented with a graphic image. The image is embedded with virtual "sensors" placed at various points. The question will ask you to identify something specific within the image or to select an answer from several listed within the image. You will indicate your selection by clicking on a virtual sensor. For example, the image could be a diagram of the human body. If the question asks where the lungs are located, you would click the chest, activating the sensor there. While hot spot questions are different from a traditional multiple-choice question, they might be easier for you to do. Clicking on part of an image—rather than selecting a choice from A to D—might feel similar to how you express knowledge in the real world.

Hot spot questions appear on every subtest except RLA. On the Mathematics subtest, hot spots are most often used to assess your ability to plot points on coordinate grids, number lines, or scatter plots. For example, the graphic image could be a coordinate grid, and the question would ask you to plot a specific point, like (5, −2). You would then click the spot on the graph associated with (5, −2). Other math questions include identifying specific parts of a scale model, selecting numerical or algebraic expressions that identify parallel equations, or identifying different representations of the same numeric value.

On the Science subtest, hot spot questions may use a graphic image or a block of text. In addition to allowing you to identify information on a model or diagram, they assess your understanding of the relationship between data points or your ability to use data points to support or refute a particular conclusion.

On the Social Studies subtest, hot spots questions often ask you to indicate evidence that supports a particular statement or idea. Like on the Science subtest, you might be asked to demonstrate the relationship between different data points from a short block of text or an image. They are also often used with mapping.

EXAMPLE

2. The square below is based on the eye color of two parents: one with brown eyes and one with green. According to this square, this couple's biological children have a 50 percent chance of having green eyes. Click the sections of the square that support this conclusion.

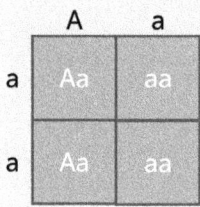

DROP-DOWN (CLOZE)

A drop-down question is an open-stem question, or incomplete statement. This type of question occurs in multiple-choice questions as well. However, in a drop-down question, rather than selecting an answer from the A – D options that appear after the statement, a drop-down box with multiple response options is embedded in the statement. You will select the appropriate word or phrase, which will fill in the blank. You can then read the complete statement to check the accuracy of your response. For example, a question might read, *Bananas are*, followed by a drop-down box with several colors listed—blue, red, yellow, green. You would click yellow, and the statement would then read, *Bananas are yellow*.

On the Mathematics subtest, drop-down questions are most often used to assess math vocabulary or to compare two quantities, in which case the drop-down box will contain less than, greater than, and equal signs. For other drop-down questions, you will be asked to select the correct number to complete a statement.

On the RLA subtest, drop-down questions are used to assess mastery of language skills, such as American English conventions, standard usage, and punctuation. Drop-down questions on this subtest mimic the editing process. So multiple variations of the same phrase will appear in the drop-down box within the text, and you will select the one that is grammatically correct. It is important to read the complete sentence after your selection to ensure your choice makes sense.

On the Science and Social Studies subtests, these questions are also most often used with text. You may be asked to draw a logical conclusion from provided text-based evidence or to make a generalization based on an author's argument.

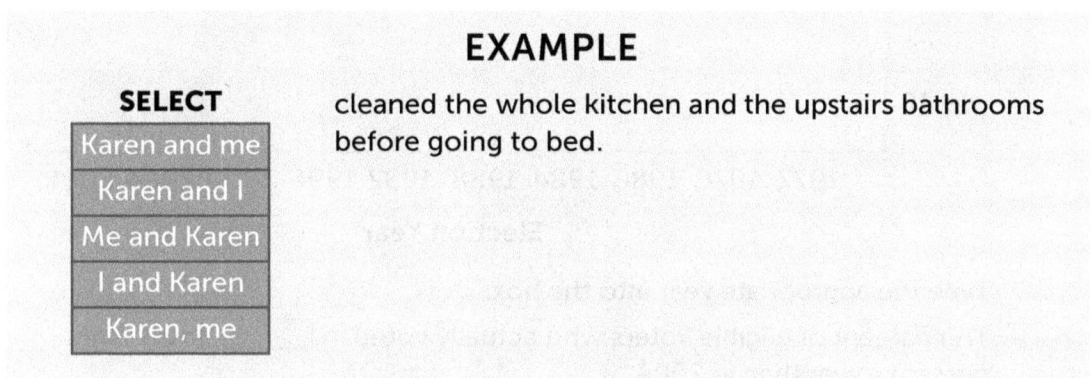

FILL-IN-THE-BLANK (FIB)

A fill-in-the-blank (FIB) question is a combination of a standard item and a constructed response. It is similar to a drop-down question in that it contains an incomplete statement. However, rather than selecting an answer from several options, you type in the answer. Unlike a constructed response, the answer you type will be only one to two words long. Using the example in the drop-down section, if the statement read, *Bananas are*, rather than selecting from several colors, you would simply type *yellow*. FIB can only be used for questions in which the answers have very little variability (so this particular example would not actually appear on the test). Sometimes a question may have more than one blank, requiring you to type two separate responses. FIB questions assess your knowledge without the distraction of incorrect choices.

FIB questions are included in all subtests except the RLA subtest. On the Mathematics subtest, FIB questions may ask you to type a numerical answer to a math problem or to write an equation using the numbers and characters on the keyboard. On the Science subtest, an FIB question may ask you to fill in the specific quantity of something from a graphic representation of data or for a response to a specific calculation.

On the Social Studies subtest, FIB questions are used to assess your understanding of a concept or key vocabulary. Often there will be brief text from which you will have to infer the concept or vocabulary. Other questions will ask you to identify specific information—from a chart, graph, or map—that supports or demonstrates a concept, idea, or trend.

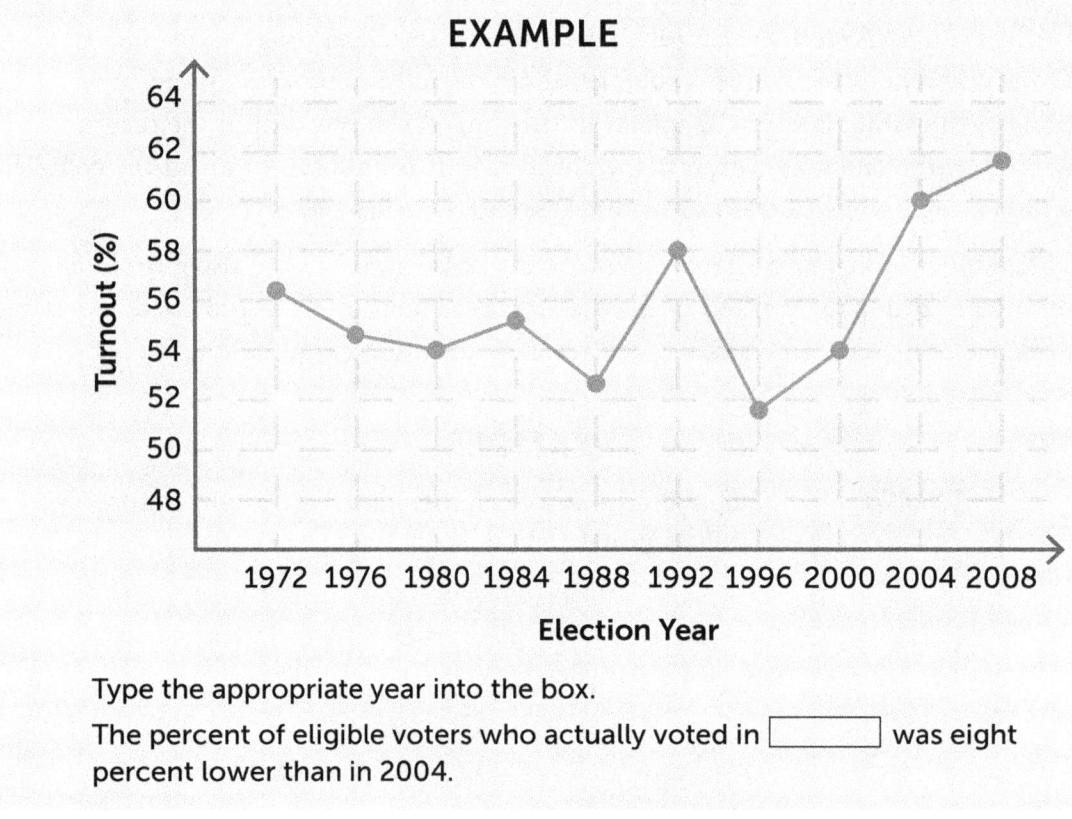

Type the appropriate year into the box.
The percent of eligible voters who actually voted in ☐ was eight percent lower than in 2004.

How is the GED Scored?

You will receive your scores on your GED tests within twenty-four hours of completing the exam.

The number of raw points each question is worth depends on the number of required answers for that question. For example, a question that requires the test-taker to select two items from a drop-down menu would be worth two raw points.

The two science constructed-response questions are scored on a three-point scale. Scores are based on scientific reasoning, the application of relevant scientific skills, and the quality of the evidence or support provided.

The written component of the Reasoning through Language Arts subtest is scored on three traits: analysis of arguments and use of evidence, development of ideas and structure, and clarity and command of standard English. Each trait can earn a raw score of up to two points.

The number of questions can vary between versions of the exam but the number of raw points remains constant. There are sixty-five raw score points on the Reasoning through Language Arts exam, forty-nine on the Mathematical Reasoning exam, forty on the Science exam, and thirty on the Social Studies exam. The total number of raw points earned is then scaled to a score between 100 and 200. You must earn at least 145 scaled score points in order to qualify for your high school equivalency credential. A score of at least 165 qualifies you as College Ready, and a score of 175 or higher qualifies you as College Ready + Credit, meaning you could qualify to receive college credit.

Each test is scored independently, and points from one test cannot affect the point value of another. You must pass each subtest in order to qualify for your high school-equivalency credential.

There is no guessing penalty on the GED exam, so you should always guess if you do not know the answer to a question.

How is the GED Administered?

The GED exam is a computer-based test offered at a wide range of sites throughout the United States and the world. To find a test center near you, check with Pearson VUE.

You will need to print your registration ticket from your online account and bring it, along with your identification, to the testing site on test day. Some test centers will require other forms or documentation, so make sure to check with your test center in advance. No pens, pencils, erasers, printed or written materials, electronic devices or calculators are allowed. An online scientific calculator will be provided to you at the time of the test as well as a formula reference sheet for the math test. Check in advance with your testing center for specific testing guidelines, including restrictions on dress and accessories.

You may take the subtests all on the same day or individually on separate days. There is no required order for completing the test. Certain jurisdictions may apply limits to the amount of time available for completing all four tests.

There are three versions of each test, so if you want to retake the test, you can do so right away up to two times. You will receive a different version of the test each time. If you still need to retake the test after the third time, you must wait sixty days. Ultimately, you may take each test up to eight times a year. If you do not pass one subtest, you are not required to retake all of the tests—only the one you failed.

About This Guide

This guide will help you to master the most important test topics and also develop critical test-taking skills. We have built features into our books to prepare you for your tests and increase your score. Along with a detailed summary of the test's format, content, and scoring, we offer an in-depth overview of the content knowledge required to pass the test. In the review you'll find sidebars that provide interesting information, highlight key concepts, and review content so that you can solidify your understanding of the exam's concepts. You can also test your knowledge with sample questions throughout the text and practice questions that reflect the content and format of the GED. We're pleased you've chosen Accepted, Inc. to be a part of your journey!

CHAPTER ONE
Scientific Practices

Scientific Inquiry

Science is defined simply as the study of the natural world. Although there are many disciplines within science, all scientific understanding is reached using a systematic gathering of observations and evidence. The investigations scientists use to gather this information can be descriptive, comparative, or experimental in nature. Once scientists conduct investigations using a range of methods and technology, they can begin to form explanations about natural phenomena. Over time, these explanations are collected in the general body of scientific knowledge and are used to form laws, or generalizations of the natural world, and theories, or explanations of laws.

SCIENTIFIC INQUIRY is defined as the myriad ways in which scientists conduct their studies and form explanations. There is no one set path that all scientists must follow, but the **SCIENTIFIC METHOD** provides a general framework for conducting scientific inquiry. The scientific method has five steps:

1. **FORM A QUESTION.**
   OBSERVATIONS about the natural world lead to questions about how or why the observed actions occur. The scientist should also do **RESEARCH** on current knowledge of the topic in the scientific community. Together, observations and research can be used to create a question to be answered.

2. **FORM A HYPOTHESIS.**
   A proposed explanation of natural phenomena is also known as a **HYPOTHESIS**. A hypothesis consists of more than an educated guess; it is a testable proposition that scientists use as the basis for an investigation. If a proposition cannot be tested scientifically, it is not a hypothesis.

3. **CONDUCT AN EXPERIMENT.**
   The next step is to design and conduct an experiment that tests the hypothesis. A scientific investigation contains an **EXPERIMENTAL VARIABLE**,

which scientists can manipulate during the course of the investigation, and **EXPERIMENTAL CONTROLS**, which are variables that are kept constant.

4. **COLLECT AND ANALYZE DATA.**
   Data should be collected during the experiment. This data can then be analyzed to look for statistically valid relationships and patterns.

5. **DRAW A CONCLUSION.**
   Finally, experimental data is used to draw conclusions about the hypothesis. The hypothesis may be proven false, or the data may support the hypothesis.

EXAMPLE

1. Which of the following best defines a hypothesis?
   A) an educated guess
   B) a study of the natural world
   C) an explanation of natural phenomena
   D) a testable proposed scientific explanation

Designing Experiments

Scientists use a rigorous set of rules to design experiments. The protocols of **EXPERIMENTAL DESIGN** are meant to ensure that scientists are actually testing what they set out to test. A well-designed experiment will measure the impact of a single factor on a system, thus allowing the experimenter to draw conclusions about that factor.

Every experiment includes variables—the factors or treatments that may affect the outcome of the experiment. **INDEPENDENT VARIABLES** are controlled by the experimenter. They are usually the factors the experimenter has hypothesized will have an effect on the system. Often, a design will include a treatment group and a **CONTROL GROUP**, which does not receive the treatment. The **DEPENDENT VARIABLES** are factors that are influenced by the independent variable.

For example, in an experiment investigating which type of fertilizer has the greatest effect on plant growth, the independent variable is the type of fertilizer used. The scientist is controlling, or manipulating, the type of fertilizer. The dependent variable is plant growth because the amount of plant growth depends on the type of fertilizer. The type of plant, the amount of water, and the amount of sunlight the plants receive are controls because those variables of the experiment are kept the same for each plant.

DID YOU KNOW?
Reproducibility is an essential feature of a scientific finding. Under the same conditions and using the same experimental methods, multiple researchers should be able to produce identical results.

When designing an experiment, scientists must identify possible sources of **EXPERIMENTAL ERROR**. These can be **CONFOUNDING**

VARIABLES—factors that act much like the independent variable and thus can make it appear that the independent variable has a greater effect than it actually does. The design may also include unknown variables that are not controlled by the scientists. Finally, scientists must be aware of **HUMAN ERROR**, particularly in collecting data and making observations, and of possible equipment errors.

> ### EXAMPLE
>
> **2.** A chemistry student is conducting an experiment in which she tests the relationship between reactant concentration and heat produced by a reaction. In her experiment, she alters the reactant concentration and measures heat produced. The independent variable in the experiment is the
>
> **A)** reactant concentration.
>
> **B)** reaction rate.
>
> **C)** amount of heat produced by the reaction.
>
> **D)** product concentration.

Facts, Theories, and Laws

Scientific facts, *theories*, and *laws* are terms with specific, distinct definitions. **SCIENTIFIC FACTS** are objective observations that have been repeatedly confirmed by **DATA** collected by multiple scientific **INVESTIGATIONS**. Facts are generally accepted as truth, but they are never considered final proof. Facts are the observations themselves, rather than the explanations for a natural phenomenon.

Explanations of natural phenomena are the realm of hypotheses and theories. Hypotheses, as earlier defined, are proposed testable explanations of natural phenomena. In order to be testable, a hypothesis must contain specific observations researchers could expect to see if the hypothesis were confirmed. Hypotheses that are tested and confirmed time and time again could eventually accumulate enough data to be considered a **THEORY**. A theory is a well-founded explanation that is supported by large amounts of data and incorporates multiple sources of evidence. Unlike the everyday definition of *theory*, which suggests just an idea, a scientific theory is widely accepted as a valid explanation of phenomena.

Unlike theories, which are *explanations* of phenomena, scientific **LAWS** are a generalized *description* of natural phenomena based on multiple observations over time. Laws are distinguished from facts by their durability—or ability to stay constant over time—and their predictive nature. If multiple investigations are run under the exact same conditions over and over, the new observations will conform to the scientific law. If results are not as predicted, then the law can be modified and narrowed to incorporate the new information.

EXAMPLE

3. Why is the germ theory of disease considered to be a theory?
   A) There is insufficient evidence to support it.
   B) Valid alternative explanations exist.
   C) It is strongly supported by existing evidence.
   D) It has only limited clinical application.

Test Your Knowledge

Read the question, and then choose the most correct answer.

1. Which of the following is the first step of the scientific method?
   A) construct a hypothesis
   B) make observations
   C) analyze data
   D) form a question

2. A woman has been suffering from heartburn and thinks that a particular food is causing it. She decides that for each week during a single month, she will not eat a specific food and see if she has heartburn that week. In her experiment, the food she removes from her diet would be which of the following types of variable?
   A) controlled variable
   B) dependent variable
   C) independent variable
   D) experimental variable

3. A scientist discovers a new species of snail that lives in the ocean. He tested the ability of this species to handle heat by measuring its growth rate as he increased the temperature of the water. He also tested two different concentrations of salt to determine which type of marine environment the snail would be best suited for.

   Which of the following is the dependent variable in the experiments described above?
   A) salt concentration
   B) temperature
   C) growth rate
   D) number of snails

4. Which of the following types of variables is changed in a scientific experiment?
   A) controlled variable
   B) measured variable
   C) dependent variable
   D) independent variable

5. A chemist plans to determine the concentration of the acid by performing an acid–base titration reaction. To perform this reaction, he adds a known volume and concentration of strong base to the acid while measuring the pH of the combined acid and base. Once a neutral pH is obtained, the reaction has proceeded to completion and the concentration of the acid may be calculated. In this reaction, what is the dependent variable?
   A) the acid concentration
   B) the volume of base added to reach reaction completion
   C) the concentration of the base
   D) the pH of the reaction mixture

6. Which of the following is a description of a natural phenomenon based on multiple observations?
   A) law
   B) theory
   C) model
   D) hypothesis

Scientific Practices

7. A chemist hypothesizes that elevating the temperature of the reaction vessel will increase the mass of product produced during a reaction. He conducts experiments to test this hypothesis and finds that the mass of product remains constant regardless of the temperature of reaction. He later discovers that the balance used to determine the masses of the product samples was calibrated incorrectly.

What step should the chemist take next?

- **A)** He should repeat the experiment because his data is flawed.
- **B)** The calibration of the scale identically affected each sample, so he can ignore the error.
- **C)** He should repeat the experiment using a different reaction vessel.
- **D)** He should estimate the true product masses based on the calibration of the balance.

8. Which of the following is an example of human error in an experiment?

- **A)** an imperfectly calibrated scale
- **B)** contaminating a sterile sample by breathing on it
- **C)** a draft in the laboratory slightly changing the temperature of a liquid
- **D)** failure to account for wind speed when measuring distance traveled

Answer Key

EXAMPLES

1. **D) is correct.** A hypothesis must be testable and propose an explanation of observed natural phenomena.

2. **A) is correct.** The independent variable is deliberately changed in the course of the experiment. Here, the student is changing the reactant concentration. The heat produced is the dependent variable.

3. **C) is correct.** A scientific theory is typically strongly supported by evidence, despite public misunderstanding to the contrary.

TEST YOUR KNOWLEDGE

1. **B) is correct.** Making observations is the first step of the scientific method; observations enable the researcher to form a question and begin the research process.

2. **C) is correct.** The independent variable is the single variable that is altered during an experiment. The woman is altering her diet to see if her heartburn (the dependent variable) is affected.

3. **C) is correct.** The growth rate is the variable that is dependent on the changes to water temperature and concentration of salt in the water.

4. **D) is correct.** The independent variable is changed by the researcher during an experiment; this change may or may not cause a direct change in the dependent variable.

5. **D) is correct.** The dependent variable is the variable that is directly measured or observed in the course of the experiment. In the case of this reaction, pH is directly measured.

6. **A) is correct.** Scientific laws, like Newton's laws of gravity or Mendel's laws of heredity, describe phenomena in the natural world that have repeatedly occurred with no known exceptions.

7. **A) is correct.** The mass data collected cannot be trusted, and the experiments should be repeated and the data collected with a properly calibrated balance.

8. **B) is correct.** Contaminating a sample by breathing on it is an example of human error, or error that occurs when the researcher makes a mistake.

Scientific Practices

CHAPTER TWO
Life Science

Biological Molecules

Molecules that contain carbon bound to hydrogen are **ORGANIC MOLECULES**. Large organic molecules that contain many atoms and repeating units are **MACROMOLECULES**. Many macromolecules are **POLYMERS** composed of repeating small units called **MONOMERS**. There are four basic biological macromolecules that are common between all organisms: carbohydrates, lipids, proteins, and nucleic acids.

CARBOHYDRATES, also called sugars, are polymers made of carbon, hydrogen, and oxygen atoms. The monomer for carbohydrates are **MONOSACCHARIDES**, such as glucose and fructose, that combine to form more complex sugars called **POLYSACCHARIDES**. Carbohydrates store energy and provide support to cellular structures.

LIPIDS, commonly known as fats, are composed mainly of hydrogen and carbon. They serve a number of functions depending on their particular structure: they make up the membrane of cells and can act as fuel, as steroids, and as hormones. Lipids are hydrophobic, meaning they repel water.

DID YOU KNOW?
An **ENZYME** is a protein that accelerates a specific chemical reaction.

PROTEINS serve an incredibly wide variety of purposes within the body. As enzymes, they play key roles in important processes like DNA replication, cellular division, and cellular metabolism. Structural proteins provide rigidity to cartilage, hair, nails, and the cytoskeletons (the network of molecules that holds the parts of a cell in place). They are also involved in communication between cells and in the transportation of molecules.

Proteins are composed of individual **AMINO ACIDS**, which are joined together by peptide bonds to form **POLYPEPTIDES**. There are twenty amino acids, and the order of the amino acids in the polypeptide determines the shape and function of the molecule.

NUCLEIC ACIDS store hereditary information and are composed of monomers called NUCLEOTIDES. Each nucleotide includes a sugar, a phosphate group, and a nitrogenous base.

There are two types of nucleic acids. **DEOXYRIBONUCLEIC ACID (DNA)** contains the genetic instructions to produce proteins. It is composed of two strings of nucleotides wound into a double helix shape. The "backbone" of the helix is made from the nucleotide's sugar (deoxyribose) and phosphate groups. The "rungs" of the ladder are made from one of four nitrogenous bases: adenine, thymine, cytosine, and guanine. These bases bond together in specific pairs: adenine with thymine and cytosine with guanine.

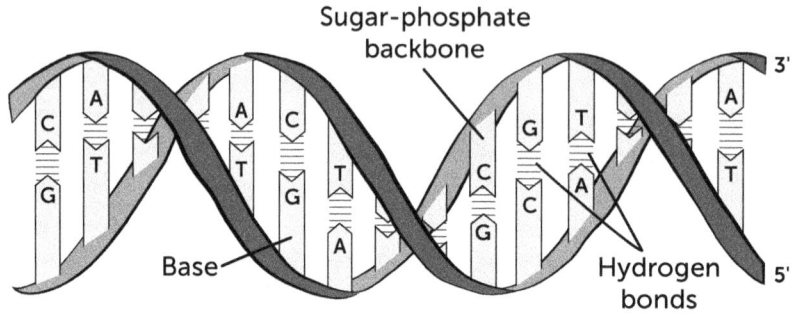

Figure 2.1. The Structure of DNA

RIBONUCLEIC ACID (RNA) transcribes information from DNA and plays several vital roles in the replication of DNA and the manufacturing of proteins. RNA nucleotides contain a sugar (ribose), a phosphate group, and one of four nitrogenous bases: adenine, uracil, cytosine, and guanine. It is usually found as a single-stranded molecule. There are three main differences between DNA and RNA:

1. DNA contains the nucleotide thymine; RNA contains the nucleotide uracil.
2. DNA is double-stranded; RNA is single-stranded.
3. DNA is made from the sugar deoxyribose; RNA is made from the sugar ribose.

EXAMPLES

1. Macromolecules are formed from small subunits called monomers. Which of the following are the monomers that make up a protein?
    A) monosaccharides
    B) nucleotides
    C) amino acids
    D) polypeptides

2. Which of the following is NOT true of RNA?
- **A)** Hydrogen bonds form between A–T and G–C bases.
- **B)** A sequence of RNA will not contain T bases but will contain U bases.
- **C)** RNA is single-stranded.
- **D)** RNA stores genetic information.

Nucleic Acids

DNA stores information by coding for proteins using blocks of three nucleotides called **CODONS**. Each codon codes for a specific amino acid; together, all the codons needed to make a specific protein are called a **GENE**. In addition to codons for specific amino acids, there are also codons that signal "start" and "stop."

The production of a protein starts with **TRANSCRIPTION**. During transcription, the two sides of the DNA helix unwind and a complementary strand of messenger RNA (mRNA) is manufactured using the DNA as a template.

This mRNA then travels outside the nucleus where it is "read" by a ribosome during **TRANSLATION**. Each codon on the mRNA is matched to an anti-codon on a strand of tRNA, which carries a specific amino acid. The amino acids bond as they are lined up next to each other, forming a polypeptide.

When it is not being transcribed, DNA is tightly wound around proteins called **HISTONES** to create **NUCLEOSOMES**, which are in turn packaged into **CHROMATIN**. The structure of chromatin allows large amounts of DNA to be stored in a very small space and helps regulate transcription by controlling access to specific sections of DNA. Tightly folding the DNA also helps prevent damage to the genetic code. Chromatin is further bundled into packages of DNA called **CHROMOSOMES**. During cell division, DNA is replicated to create two identical copies of each chromosome called **CHROMATIDS**.

Somatic (body) cells are **DIPLOID**, meaning they carry two copies of each chromosome—one inherited from each parent. Gametes, which are reproductive cells, are **HAPLOID** and carry only one copy of each chromosome. Human somatic cells have forty-six chromosomes, while human egg and sperm each carry twenty-three chromosomes.

A **MUTATION** causes a change in the sequence of nucleotides within DNA. For example, the codon GAC codes for the amino acid aspartic acid. However, if the cytosine is swapped for adenine, the codon now reads GAA, which corresponds to the amino acid glutamic acid. Germ-line mutations, or mutations that occur in a cell that will become a gamete, can be passed on to the offspring of an organism. Somatic mutations cannot be passed on to the offspring of an organism.

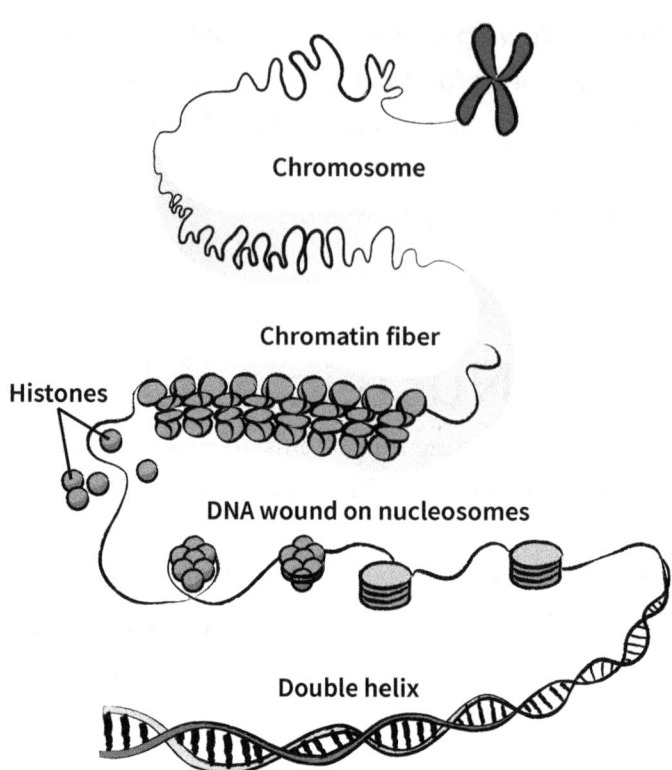

Figure 2.2. DNA, Chromatin, and Chromosomes

EXAMPLE

3. Which of the following processes uses the information stored in RNA to produce a protein?
   A) replication
   B) translation
   C) transcription
   D) mutation

Structure and Function of Cells

A CELL is the smallest unit of life that can reproduce on its own. Unicellular organisms, such as amoebae, are made up of only one cell, while multicellular organisms are comprised of many cells. There are two basic types of cells: prokaryotic and eukaryotic. PROKARYOTIC CELLS, which include most bacteria, do not have a nucleus. The DNA in a prokaryotic cell is carried in the CYTOPLASM, which is the fluid that makes up the volume of the cell. EUKARYOTIC CELLS contain a nucleus where genetic material is stored.

Cells contain smaller structures called ORGANELLES that perform specific functions within the cell. These include MITOCHONDRIA, which produce energy; RIBOSOMES, which produce proteins; and VACUOLES, which store water and other molecules.

Plant cells include a number of structures not found in animal cells. These include the **CELL WALL**, which provides the cell with a hard outer structure, and **CHLOROPLASTS**, where photosynthesis occurs.

The outer surface of human cells is made up of a **PLASMA MEMBRANE**, which gives the cell its shape. This membrane is primarily composed of a **PHOSPHOLIPID BILAYER**, which itself is made up of two layers of lipids that face opposing directions. This functions to separate the inner cellular environment from the extracellular space, the space between cells. Molecules travel through the cell membrane using a number of different methods:

- **DIFFUSION** occurs when molecules pass through the membrane from areas of high to low concentration.
- **FACILITATED DIFFUSION** occurs with the assistance of proteins embedded in the membrane.
- **OSMOSIS** is the movement of water from areas of high to low concentration.
- During **ACTIVE TRANSPORT**, proteins in the membrane use energy (in the form of ATP) to move molecules across the membrane.

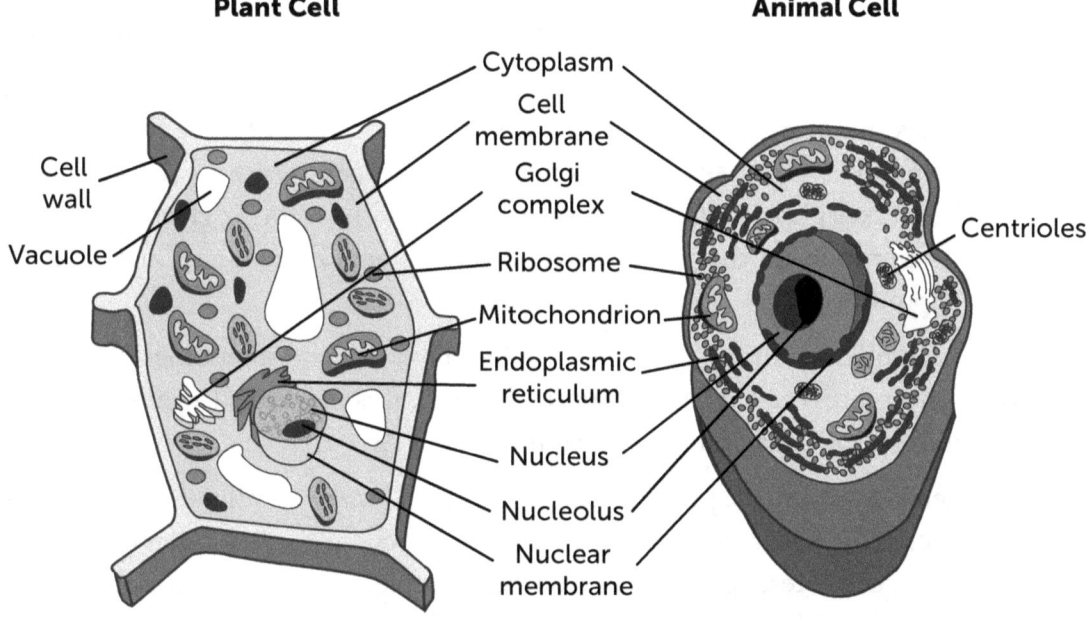

Figure 2.3. Cell Organelles

EXAMPLES

4. Which of the following structures produces proteins and is found in both prokaryotic and eukaryotic cells?
   A) nucleus
   B) chloroplast
   C) ribosome
   D) vacuole

5. The chromosomes of a eukaryotic organism would be found in the
   A) chloroplast.
   B) nucleus.
   C) mitochondria.
   D) cytoplasm.

Cellular Respiration

Organisms use chains of chemical reactions called **BIOCHEMICAL PATHWAYS** to acquire, store, and use energy. The molecule most commonly used to store energy is **ADENOSINE TRIPHOSPHATE (ATP)**. When a phosphate group (Pi) is removed from ATP, creating **ADENOSINE DIPHOSPHATE (ADP)**, energy is released. The cell harnesses this energy to perform processes such as transport, growth, and replication.

Cells also transfer energy using the molecules **NICOTINAMIDE ADENINE DINUCLEOTIDE PHOSPHATE (NADPH)** and **NICOTINAMIDE ADENINE DINUCLEOTIDE (NADH)**. These molecules are generally used to carry energy-rich electrons during the process of creating ATP.

In **CELLULAR RESPIRATION**, food molecules such as glucose are broken down, and the electrons harvested from these molecules are used to make ATP. The first stage of cellular respiration is an **ANAEROBIC** (does not require oxygen) process called **GLYCOLYSIS**. Glycolysis takes place in the cytoplasm of a cell and transforms glucose into two molecules of pyruvate. In the process, two molecules of ATP and two molecules of NADH are produced.

Under anaerobic conditions, pyruvate is reduced to acids and sometimes gases and/or alcohols in a process called **FERMENTATION**. However, this process is less efficient than aerobic cellular respiration and produces only two ATP.

Under aerobic conditions, pyruvate enters the second stage of cellular respiration—the **KREBS CYCLE**. The Krebs cycle takes place in the mitochondria, or tubular organelles, of a eukaryotic cell. Here, pyruvate is oxidized completely to form six molecules of carbon dioxide (CO_2). This set of reactions also produces two more molecules of ATP, ten molecules of NADH, and two molecules of $FADH_2$ (an electron carrier).

The electrons carried by NADH and $FADH_2$ are transferred to the **ELECTRON TRANSPORT CHAIN**, where they cascade through carrier molecules embedded in the inner mitochondrial membrane. Oxygen is the final electron receptor in the chain; it reacts with these electrons and hydrogen to form water. This sequential movement of electrons drives the formation of a proton (H^+) gradient, which is used by the enzyme ATP synthase to produce ATP. The electron transport chain produces thirty to thirty-two molecules of ATP.

The balanced chemical equation for cellular respiration is:

$$C_6H_{12}O_6 + 6O_2 \rightarrow 6CO_2 + 6H_2O$$

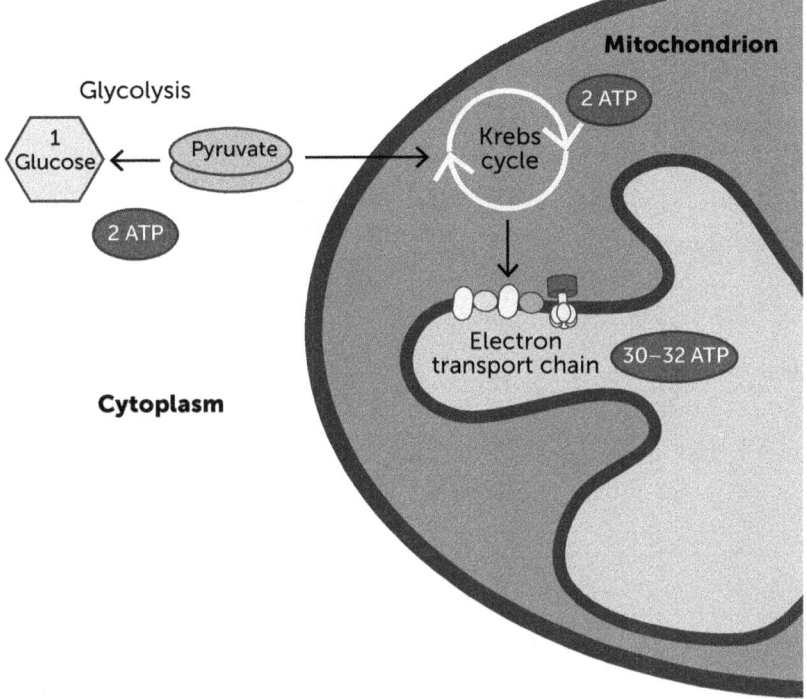

Figure 2.4. Cellular Respiration

EXAMPLE

6. Which of the following stages of cellular respiration produces the largest number of ATP molecules?
   A) glycolysis
   B) fermentation
   C) Krebs cycle
   D) electron transport chain

Photosynthesis

The sun powers nearly all biological systems on this planet. Plants, along with some bacteria and algae, harness the energy of sunlight and transform it into chemical energy through the process of **PHOTOSYNTHESIS**.

Inside each chloroplast are stacks of flat, interconnected sacs called **THYLAKOIDS**. Within the membrane of each thylakoid sac are light-absorbing pigments called **CHLOROPHYLL**.

In the light-dependent reactions of photosynthesis, light penetrates the chloroplast and strikes the chlorophyll. The energy in the sunlight excites electrons, boosting them to a higher energy level. These excited electrons then cascade through the **ELECTRON TRANSPORT CHAIN**, creating energy in the form of ATP and NADPH. This reaction also splits water to release O_2.

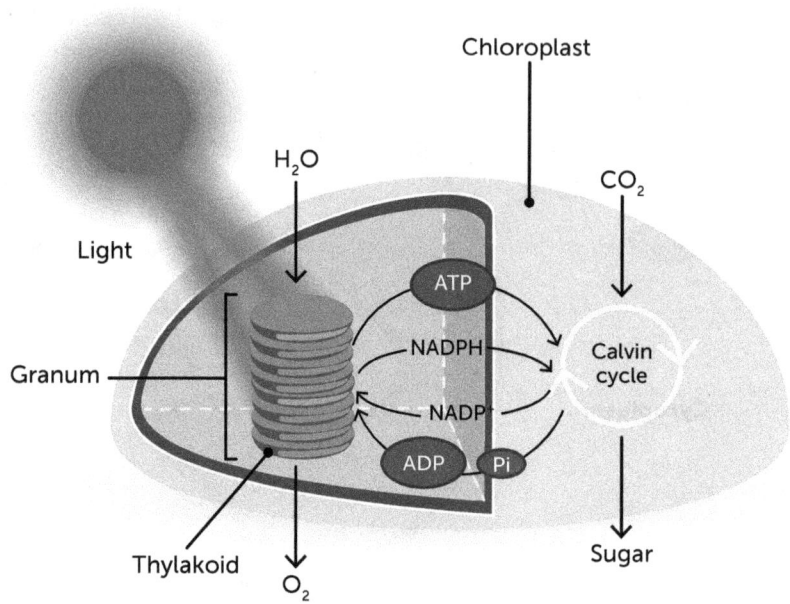

Figure 2.5. Photosynthesis

The ATP and NADPH created by the light-dependent stage of photosynthesis enters the **Calvin cycle**, which uses the energy to produce the carbohydrate glucose ($C_6H_{12}O_6$). The carbon needed for this reaction comes from atmospheric CO_2.

The balanced chemical equation for photosynthesis is:

$$6CO_2 + 6H_2O \rightarrow C_6H_{12}O_6 + 6O_2$$

EXAMPLE

7. All of the following molecules are used in the Calvin cycle EXCEPT
- **A)** O_2.
- **B)** CO_2.
- **C)** ATP.
- **D)** NADPH.

Cell Division

The process of cell growth and reproduction is the **cell cycle**. Eukaryotic cells spend the majority of their lifespan in **interphase**, during which the cell performs necessary functions and grows. During interphase, the cell also copies its DNA. Then, during **mitosis** the two identical sets of DNA are pulled to opposite sides of the cell. The cell then splits during **cytokinesis**, resulting in two cells that have identical copies of the original cell's DNA.

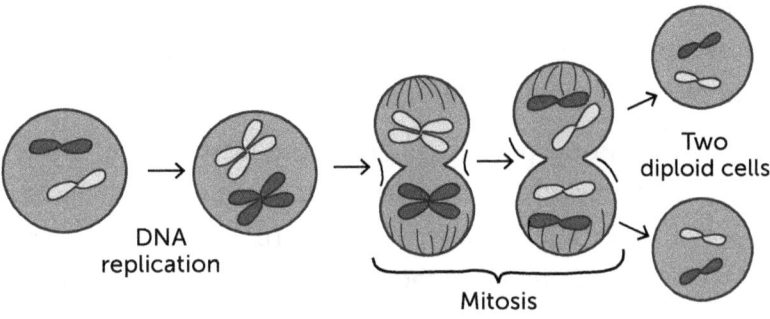

Figure 2.6. Mitosis

MEIOSIS is the process of sexual reproduction, or the formation of gametes (egg and sperm cells). During meiosis, the replicated DNA is separated to form two diploid cells. These cells in turn will separate again, with each cell retaining a single set of chromosomes. The result is four haploid cells.

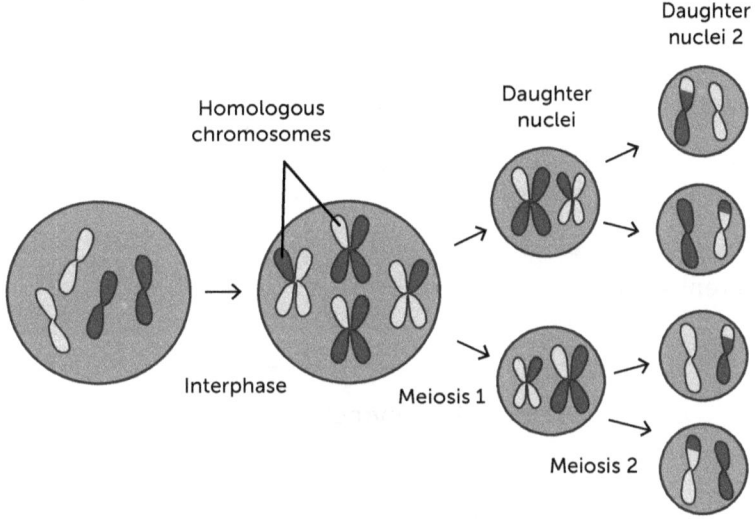

Figure 2.7. Meiosis

EXAMPLE

8. The result of mitosis and cytokinesis is
   A) two haploid cells.
   B) four haploid cells.
   C) two diploid cells.
   D) four diploid cells.

Genetics

GENETICS is the study of heredity—how characteristics are passed from parents to offspring. These characteristics, or traits, are determined by genes. Each individual has two versions of the same gene, called **ALLELES**, with one contributed by each parent. An individual is **HOMOZYGOUS** for a particular gene if both alleles are the same, and **HETEROZYGOUS** if the two alleles are different.

DID YOU KNOW?
Alleles are written as a single letter with the dominant allele capitalized (A) and the recessive allele lowercase (a).

For a particular gene, the **DOMINANT** allele will always be expressed, and the **RECESSIVE** allele will only be expressed if the other allele is also recessive. In other words, a recessive trait is only expressed if the individual is homozygous for that allele.

The full set of genetic material in an organism is its **GENOTYPE**. The organism's **PHENOTYPE** is the set of observable traits in the organism. For example, brown hair is a phenotype. The genotype of this trait is a set of alleles that contain the genetic information for brown hair.

The genotype, and resulting phenotype, of sexually reproducing organisms can be tracked using **PUNNETT SQUARES**, which show the alleles of the parent generation on each of two axes. The possible genotype of the resulting offspring, called the F1 generation, are then shown in the body of the square.

Parent #1: Rr

	R	r
R	RR	Rr
r	Rr	rr

Parent #2: Rr

Figure 2.8. Punnett Square

In Figure 2.8., two heterozygous parents for trait R are mated, resulting in the following genotypes and phenotypes for the offspring:

- ▶ 1 homozygous dominant (dominant phenotype)
- ▶ 2 heterozygous (dominant phenotype)
- ▶ 1 homozygous recessive (recessive phenotype)

DID YOU KNOW?
Many of the rules of genetics were discovered by Gregor Mendel, a nineteenth century abbot who used pea plants to show how traits are passed down through generations.

Non-Mendelian inheritance describes patterns that do not follow the ratios described above. These patterns can occur for a number of reasons. Alleles might show **INCOMPLETE DOMINANCE**, where one allele is not fully expressed over the other, resulting in a third phenotype (for example, a red flower and white flower cross to create a pink flower). Alleles can also be **CODOMINANT**, meaning both are fully expressed (such as the AB blood type).

The expression of genes can also be regulated by mechanisms other than the dominant/recessive relationship. For example, some genes may inhibit the expression of other genes, a process called **EPISTASIS**. The environment can also impact gene expression. For example, organisms with the same genotype may grow to different sizes depending on the nutrients available to them.

EXAMPLES

9. Which of the following is NOT a scenario in which the dominant allele will be expressed as a trait?
    A) a recessive allele from the father paired with a recessive allele from the mother
    B) a dominant allele from the father paired with a dominant allele from the mother
    C) a dominant allele from the father paired with a recessive allele from the mother
    D) a recessive allele from the father paired with a dominant allele from the mother

10. Alleles for brown eyes (B) are dominant over alleles for blue eyes (b). If two parents are both heterozygous for this gene, what is the percent chance that their offspring will have brown eyes?
    A) 25
    B) 50
    C) 75
    D) 100

Evolution

EVOLUTION is the gradual genetic change in species over time. Natural selection alters the variation and frequency of certain alleles and phenotypes within a population. This increased variation and frequency leads to varying reproductive success, in which individuals with certain traits survive over others. Combined, these mechanisms lead to a gradual changes in the genotype of individual populations that, over time, can result in the creation of a new species.

NATURAL SELECTION is a process in which only the members of a population best adapted to their environment tend to survive and reproduce, which ensures that their favorable traits will be passed on to future generations of the species. There are four basic conditions that must be met in order for natural selection to occur:

1. inherited variation
2. overproduction of offspring
3. fitness to environment
4. differential reproduction

DID YOU KNOW?
Why might a harmful mutation continue to exist in a population?

The offspring with inherited variations best suited for their environment will be more likely to survive than others and are therefore more likely to pass on their successful genes to future populations through reproduction. This is referred to as **fitness**. An organism that is considered biologically "fit" will be more successful passing on its genes through reproduction compared to other members of the population. The frequency of certain alleles in a gene pool will change as a result.

Artificial selection occurs in a species when humans get involved in the reproductive process. Over time, humans have intentionally bred organisms with the same desirable traits in a process called selective breeding. This has led to the evolution of many common crops and farm animals that are bred specifically for human consumption, as well as among domesticated animals, such as horses or dogs.

EXAMPLE

11. Which of the following is NOT an example of natural selection?
    A) peahens selecting the most brightly colored peacocks as mates
    B) large bears chasing smaller rivals away from food sources
    C) sparrows with a certain beak shape reaching plentiful food sources
    D) farmers planting seeds only from the most productive corn plants

Ecology

Ecology is the study of organisms' interactions with each other and the environment. Ecologists break down the groups of organisms and abiotic features into hierarchal groups.

Groups of organisms of the same species living in the same geographic area are called **populations**. These organisms will compete with each other for resources and mates and will display characteristic patterns in growth related to their interactions with the environment. For example, many populations exhibit a carrying capacity, which is the highest number of individuals that the resources in a given environment can support. Populations that outgrow their carrying capacity are likely to experience increased death rates until the population reaches a stable level again.

Populations of different species living together in the same geographic region are called **communities**. Within a community there are many different interactions among individuals of different species. **Predators** consume **prey** for food, and some species are in **competition** for the same limited pool of resources. In a **symbiotic** relationship, two species have evolved to share a close relationship. Two species may also have a **parasitic** relationship in which one organism benefits to the detriment of the other, such as ticks feeding off a dog. Both species benefit in a **mutualistic** relationship, and in a **commensalistic** relationship, one species benefits and the other feels the effects.

Within a community, a species exists in a **FOOD WEB**: every species either consumes or is consumed by another (or others). The lowest trophic level in the web is occupied by **PRODUCERS**, which include plants and algae that produce energy directly from the sun. The next level are **PRIMARY CONSUMERS** (herbivores), which consume plant matter. The next trophic level includes **SECONDARY CONSUMERS** (carnivores), which consume herbivores.

A food web may also contain another level of **TERTIARY CONSUMERS** (carnivores that consume other carnivores). In a real community, these webs can be extremely complex, with species existing on multiple trophic levels. Communities also include **DECOMPOSERS**, which are organisms that break down dead matter.

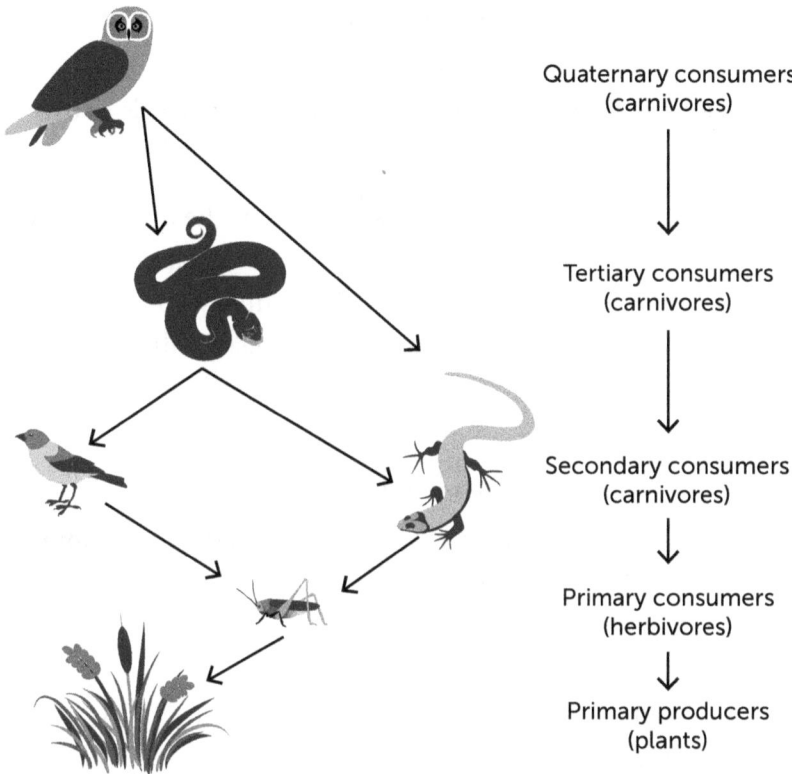

Figure 2.9. Food Web

The collection of biotic (living) and abiotic (nonliving) features in a geographic area is called an **ECOSYSTEM**. For example, in a forest, the ecosystem consists of all the organisms (animals, plants, fungi, bacteria, etc.), in addition to the soil, groundwater, rocks, and other abiotic features.

BIOMES are collections of plant and animal communities that exist within specific climates. They are similar to ecosystems, but they do not include abiotic components and can exist within and across continents. For example, the Amazon rainforest is a specific ecosystem, while tropical rainforests in general are considered a biome that includes a set of similar communities across the world. Together, all the living and nonliving parts of the earth are known as the **BIOSPHERE**.

Terrestrial biomes are usually defined by distinctive patterns in temperature and rainfall, and aquatic biomes are defined by the type of water and organisms found there. Examples of biomes include:

- **DESERTS:** extreme temperatures and very low rainfall with specialized vegetation and small mammals
- **TROPICAL RAINFORESTS:** hot and wet with an extremely high diversity of species
- **TEMPERATE GRASSLANDS:** moderate precipitation and distinct seasons with grasses and shrubs dominating
- **TEMPERATE FORESTS:** moderate precipitation and temperatures with deciduous trees dominating
- **TUNDRA:** extremely low temperatures and short growing seasons with little or no tree growth
- **CORAL REEFS:** a marine (saltwater) system with high levels of diversity
- **LAKE:** an enclosed body of fresh water

If the delicate balance of an ecosystem is disrupted, the system may not function properly. For example, if all the secondary consumers disappear, the population of primary consumers would increase, causing the primary consumers to overeat the producers and eventually starve. **KEYSTONE SPECIES** are especially important in a particular community, and removing them decreases the overall diversity of the ecosystem.

EXAMPLES

12. Which of the following is an example of an abiotic environmental factor that influences population size?
    A) food availability
    B) rate of precipitation
    C) interspecific competition
    D) competition

13. Which of the following terrestrial biomes is characterized by moderate rainfall and the dominance of deciduous trees?
    A) desert
    B) tropical rainforest
    C) temperate forest
    D) tundra

Human Anatomy and Physiology

In a multicellular organism, cells are grouped together into **TISSUES**, and these tissues are grouped into **ORGANS**, which perform specific **FUNCTIONS**. The heart, for example, is the organ that pumps blood throughout the body. Organs are further grouped into ORGAN SYSTEMS, such as the digestive or respiratory systems.

ANATOMY is the study of the structure of organisms, and PHYSIOLOGY is the study of how these structures function. Both disciplines study the systems that allow organisms to perform a number of crucial functions, including the exchange of energy, nutrients, and waste products with the environment. This exchange allows organisms to maintain HOMEOSTASIS, or the stabilization of internal conditions.

> **DID YOU KNOW?**
> In science, a **system** is a collection of interconnected parts that make up a complex whole with defined boundaries. Systems may be closed, meaning nothing passes in or out of them, or open, meaning they have inputs and outputs.

The human body has a number of systems that perform vital functions, including the digestive, excretory, respiratory, circulatory, skeletal, muscular, immune, nervous, endocrine, and reproductive systems.

The DIGESTIVE SYSTEM breaks food down into nutrients for use by the body's cells. Food enters through the MOUTH and moves through the ESOPHAGUS to the STOMACH, where it is physically and chemically broken down. The food particles then move into the SMALL INTESTINE, where the majority of nutrients are absorbed. Finally, the remaining

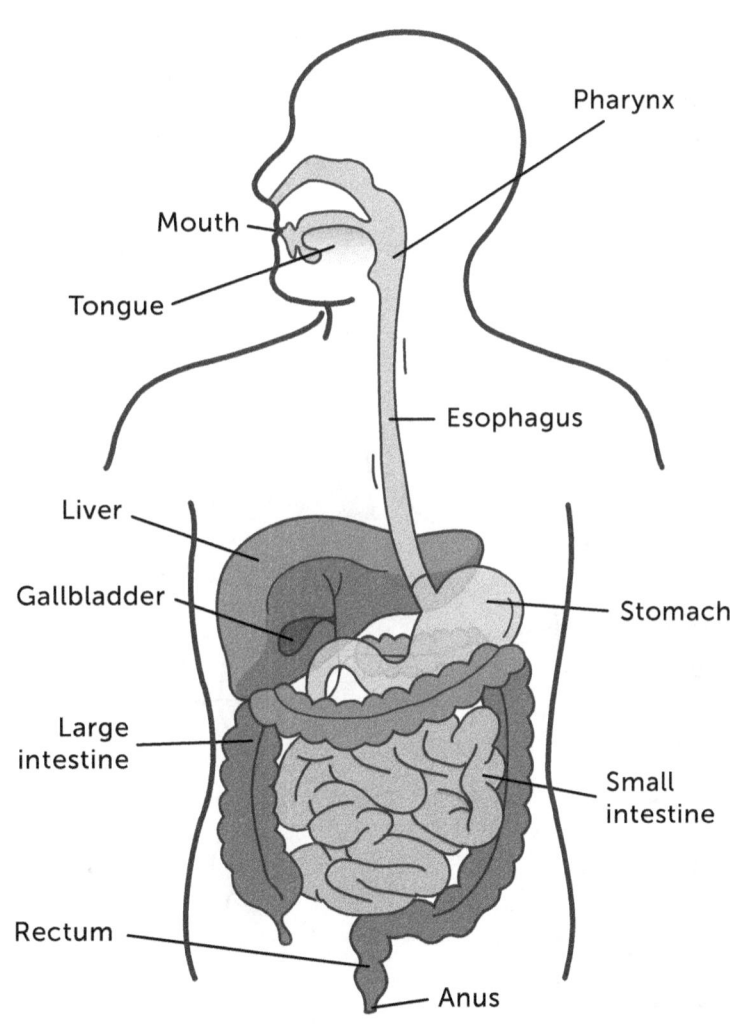

Figure 2.10. The Digestive System

particles enter the LARGE INTESTINE, which mostly absorbs water, and waste exits through the RECTUM and ANUS. This system also includes other organs, such as the LIVER, GALLBLADDER, and PANCREAS, that manufacture substances needed for digestion.

The GENITOURINARY SYSTEM removes waste products from the body. Its organs include the liver, which breaks down harmful substances, and the KIDNEYS, which filter waste from the bloodstream. The excretory system also includes the BLADDER and URINARY TRACT, which expel the waste filtered by the kidneys; the lungs, which expel the carbon dioxide created by cellular metabolism; and the skin, which secretes salt in the form of perspiration.

The RESPIRATORY SYSTEM takes in oxygen (which is needed for cellular functioning) and expels carbon dioxide. Humans take in air primarily through the nose but also through the mouth. This air travels down the TRACHEA and BRONCHI into the LUNGS, which are composed of millions of small structures called alveoli that allow for the exchange of gases between the blood and the air.

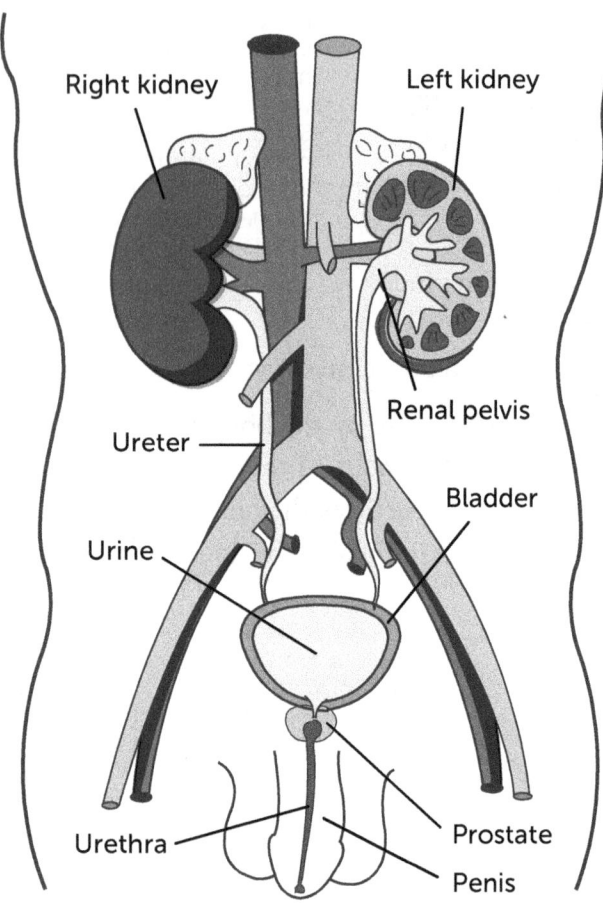

Figure 2.11. Genitourinary System

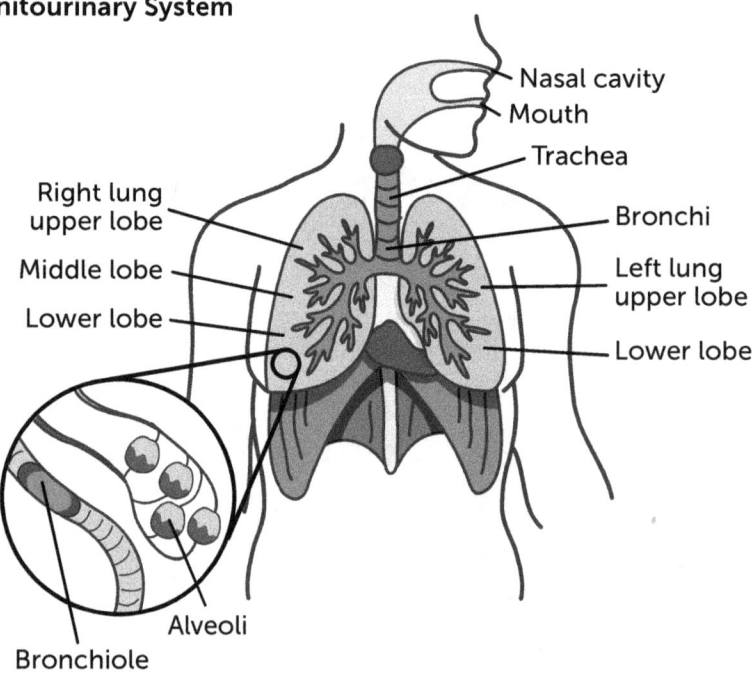

Figure 2.12. Respiratory System

The circulatory system carries oxygen, nutrients, and waste products in the blood to and from all the cells of the body. The **HEART** is a four-chambered muscle that pumps blood throughout the body. The four chambers are the right atrium, right ventricle, left atrium, and left ventricle. Deoxygenated blood (blood from which all the oxygen has been extracted and used) enters the right atrium and then is sent from the right ventricle through the pulmonary artery to the lungs, where it collects oxygen. The oxygen-rich blood then returns to the left atrium of the heart and is pumped out the left ventricle to the rest of the body.

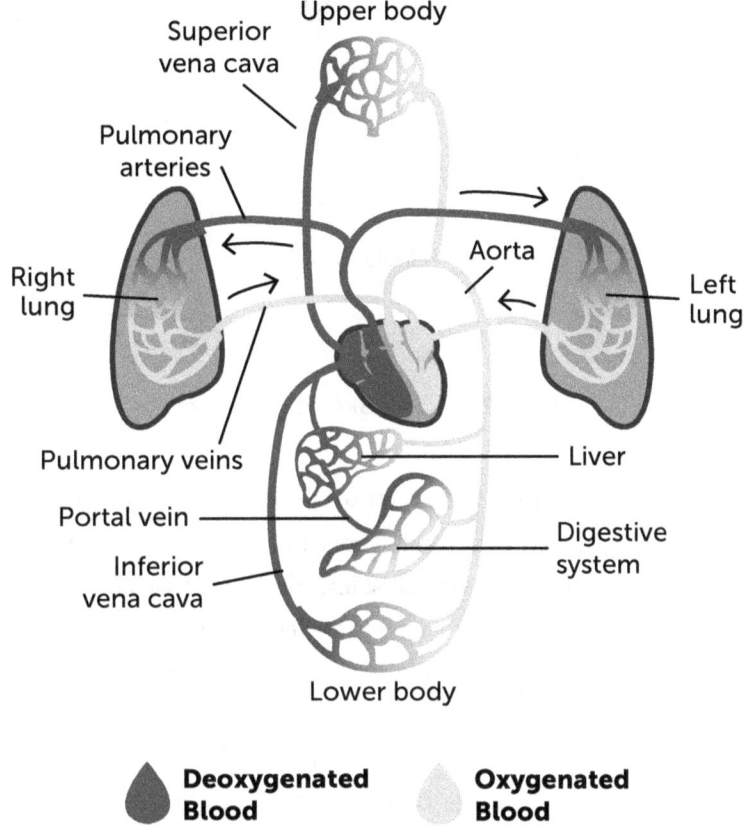

Figure 2.13. Circulatory System

Blood travels through a system of vessels. **ARTERIES** branch directly off the heart and carry blood away from it. The largest artery is the aorta, which carries blood from the heart to the rest of the body. **VEINS** carry blood back to the heart from other parts of the body. Most veins carry deoxygenated blood, but the pulmonary veins carry oxygenated blood from the lungs back to the heart to then be pumped to the rest of the body. Arteries and veins branch into smaller and smaller vessels until they become **CAPILLARIES**, which are the smallest vessels and the site where gas exchange occurs.

The **SKELETAL SYSTEM**, which is composed of the body's **BONES** and **JOINTS**, provides support for the body and helps with movement. Bones also store some of the body's nutrients and produce specific types of cells. Humans are born with 237 bones. However, many of these bones fuse during childhood, and adults have only 206 bones.

Bones can have a rough or smooth texture and come in four basic shapes: long, flat, short, and irregular.

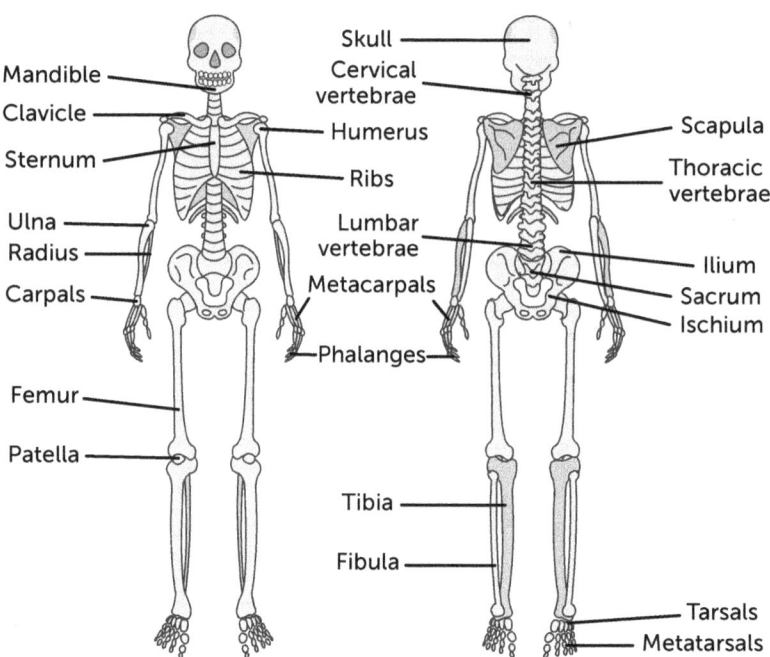

Figure 2.14. The Skeletal System

DID YOU KNOW?
Some skeletal muscles, such as the diaphragm and those that control blinking, can be voluntarily controlled but usually operate involuntarily.

The **MUSCULAR SYSTEM** allows the body to move and also moves blood and other substances through the body. The human body has three types of muscles. Skeletal muscles are voluntary muscles (meaning they can be controlled) that are attached to bones and move the body. Smooth muscles are involuntary muscles (meaning they cannot be controlled) that create movement in parts of the digestive tract, blood vessels, and the reproduction system. Finally, cardiac muscle is the involuntary muscle that contracts the heart, pumping blood throughout the body.

The **IMMUNE SYSTEM** protects the body from infection by foreign particles and organisms. It includes the **SKIN** and mucous membranes, which act as physical barriers, and a number of specialized cells that destroy foreign substances in the body. The human body has an adaptive immune system, meaning it can recognize and respond to foreign substances once it has been exposed to them. This is the underlying mechanism behind vaccines.

DID YOU KNOW?
Memory B cells are the underlying mechanisms behind vaccines, which introduce a harmless version of a pathogen into the body to activate the body's adaptive immune response.

The immune system is composed of **B CELLS**, or B lymphocytes, that produce special proteins called **ANTIBODIES** that bind to foreign substances, called **ANTIGENS**, and neutralize them. **T CELLS**, or T lymphocytes, remove body cells that have been infected by foreign invaders like bacteria or viruses. **HELPER T CELLS** coordinate production of antibodies by B cells and removal of infected cells by T cells. **KILLER T CELLS** destroy body cells that have been infected by invaders after they are identified and removed by T cells. Finally, **MEMORY CELLS** remember antigens that have been removed so the immune system can respond more quickly if they enter the body again.

The **NERVOUS SYSTEM** processes external stimuli and sends signals throughout the body. It is made up of two parts. The central nervous system (CNS) includes the brain and spinal cord and is where information is processed and stored. The brain has three parts: the cerebrum, cerebellum, and medulla. The **CEREBRUM** is the biggest part of the brain, the wrinkly gray part at the front and top, and controls different functions like thinking, vision, hearing, touch, and smell. The **CEREBELLUM** is located at the back and bottom of the brain and controls motor movements. The **MEDULLA**, or brain stem, is where the brain connects to the spinal cord and controls automatic body functions like breathing and heartbeat.

The peripheral nervous system (PNS) includes small cells called **NEURONS** that transmit information throughout the body using electrical signals. Neurons are made up of three basic parts: the cell body, dendrites, and axons. The cell body is the main part of the cell where the organelles are located. Dendrites are long arms that extend from the main cell body and communicate with other cells' dendrites through chemical messages passed across a space called a synapse. Axons are extensions from the cell body and transmit messages to the muscles.

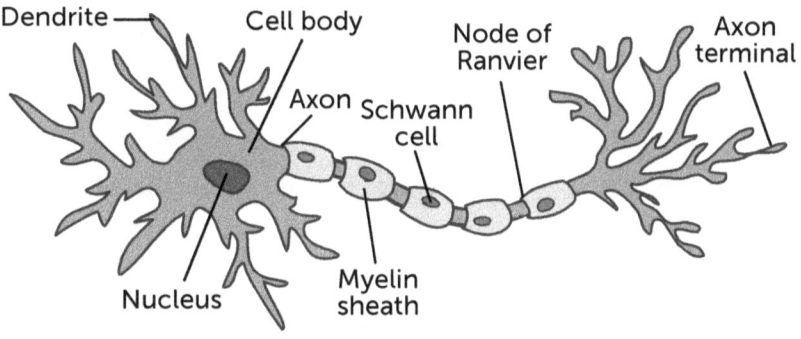

Figure 2.15. Neuron

The **ENDOCRINE SYSTEM** is a collection of organs that produce **HORMONES**, which are chemicals that regulate bodily processes. These organs include the pituitary gland, hypothalamus, pineal gland, thyroid gland, parathyroid glands, adrenal glands, testes (in males), ovaries (in females), and the placenta (in pregnant females). Together, the hormones these organs produce regulate a wide variety of bodily functions, including hunger, sleep, mood, reproduction, and temperature. Some organs that are part of other systems can also act as endocrine organs, including the pancreas and liver.

The reproductive system includes the organs necessary for sexual reproduction. In males, sperm is produced in the **TESTES** (also known as **TESTICLES**) and carried through a thin tube called the **VAS DEFERENS** to the **URETHRA**, which carries sperm through the **PENIS** and out of the body. The **PROSTATE** is a muscular gland approximately the size of a walnut that is located between the male bladder and penis and produces a fluid that nourishes and protects sperm.

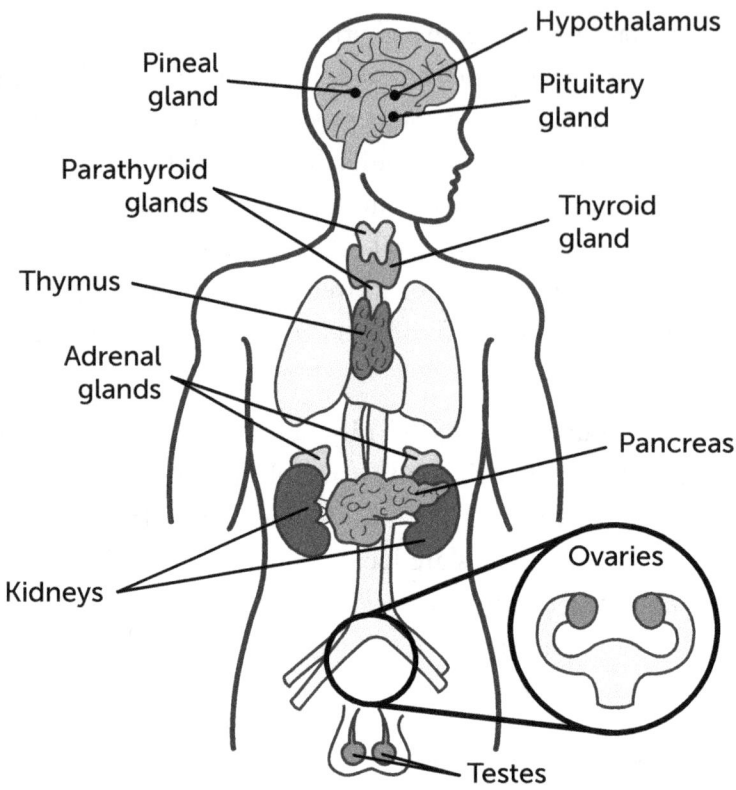

Figure 2.16. Endocrine System

In the female reproductive system, eggs are produced in the **OVARIES** and released roughly once a month to move through the **FALLOPIAN TUBES** to the **UTERUS**. If an egg is fertilized, the new embryo implants in the lining of the uterus and develops over the course of about nine months. At the end of **GESTATION**, the baby leaves the uterus

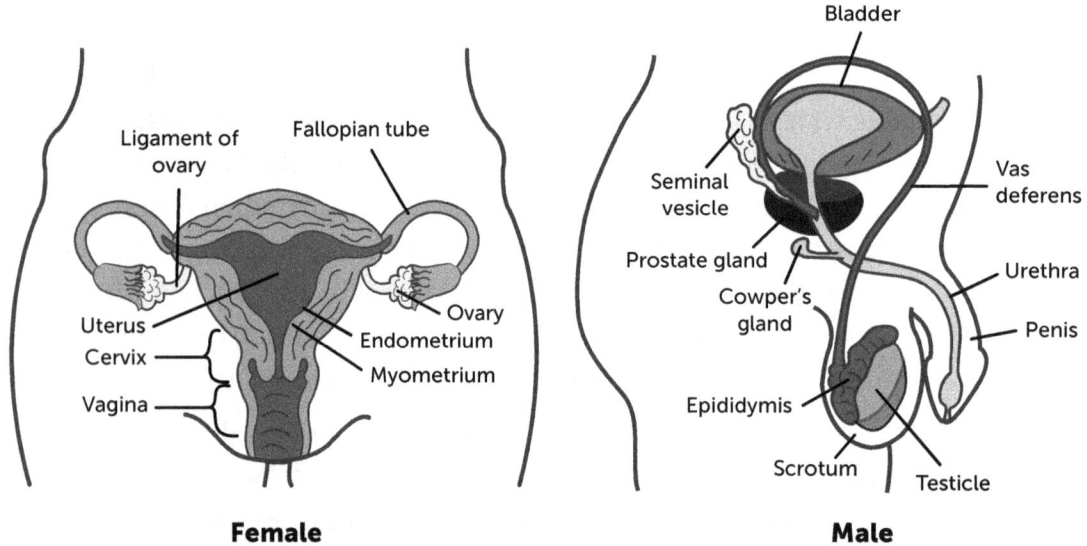

Figure 2.17. Reproductive System

through the cervix, and exits the body through the VAGINA. If the egg is not fertilized, the uterus will shed its lining.

EXAMPLES

14. Which of the following structures are small air sacs that function as the site of gas exchange in the lungs?
- **A)** capillaries
- **B)** bronchi
- **C)** alveoli
- **D)** cilia

15. Where in the digestive tract are most of the nutrients absorbed?
- **A)** small intestine
- **B)** rectum
- **C)** stomach
- **D)** large intestine

Test Your Knowledge

Read the question, and then choose the most correct answer.

1. Which of the following is NOT a nucleobase of DNA?
   A) adenine
   B) guanine
   C) thymine
   D) uracil

2. Which of the following is a monomer used to build carbohydrates?
   A) glucose
   B) thymine
   C) aspartic acid
   D) histone

3. Which of the following processes uses the information stored in RNA to produce a protein?
   A) replication
   B) translation
   C) transcription
   D) mutation

4. The information stored in DNA is used to make which of the following molecules?
   A) amino acids
   B) proteins
   C) fatty acids
   D) monosaccharides

5. Which of the following is NOT present in an animal cell?
   A) nucleus
   B) mitochondria
   C) cytoplasm
   D) cell wall

6. Which of the following cell organelles are the site of lipid synthesis?
   A) smooth endoplasmic reticulum
   B) ribosome
   C) rough endoplasmic reticulum
   D) Golgi apparatus

7. Which of the following cellular processes does NOT use ATP?
   A) facilitated diffusion
   B) DNA replication
   C) active transport through the cell membrane
   D) movement of the mot complex in a flagellum

8. Which of the following molecules can be found in abundance in a fatigued muscle?
   A) glucose
   B) lactic acid
   C) ATP
   D) myoglobin

9. Why do some photosynthetic structures, like leaves, appear green?
   A) The epidermis of the leaf absorbs red and blue light.
   B) The epidermis of the leaf absorbs green light.
   C) The chlorophyll of the leaf absorbs red and blue light.
   D) The chlorophyll of the leaf absorbs green light.

10. The Calvin cycle produces one molecule of glucose from which of the following three molecules?
    A) ATP, NADPH, and O_2
    B) ATP, NADPH, and CO_2
    C) CO_2, H_2O, and ATP
    D) CO_2, H_2O, and O_2

11. The result of meiosis and cytokinesis is
    A) two haploid (1n) cells.
    B) four haploid (1n) cells.
    C) two diploid (2n) cells.
    D) four diploid (2n) cells.

12. Alleles for brown eyes (B) are dominant over alleles for blue eyes (b). If two parents are both heterozygous for this gene, what is the percent chance that their offspring will have brown eyes?
    A) 25
    B) 50
    C) 75
    D) 100

13. If a plant that is homozygous dominant (T) for a trait is crossed with a plant that is homozygous recessive (t) for the same trait, what will be the phenotype of the offspring if the trait follows Mendelian patterns of inheritance?
    A) All offspring will show the dominant phenotype.
    B) All offspring will show the recessive phenotype.
    C) Half the offspring will show the dominant trait, and the other half will show the recessive phenotype.
    D) All the offspring will show a mix of the dominant and recessive phenotypes.

14. A female who carries the recessive color blindness gene mates with a color-blind male, resulting in a male child. Which of the following numbers represents the likelihood the offspring will also be color blind?
    A) 25 percent
    B) 50 percent
    C) 100 percent
    D) 0 percent

15. Type AB blood—the expression of both A and B antigens on a red blood cell surface—occurs as the result of which of the following?
    A) incomplete dominance
    B) recombination
    C) codominance
    D) independent assortment

16. Which of the following is NOT a condition of natural selection?
    A) differential reproduction
    B) competition between species
    C) overproduction of offspring
    D) inheritance of traits

17. A barnacle is attached to the outside of the whale to collect and consume particulate matter as the whale moves through the ocean. The barnacle benefits, while the whale is unaffected.

    The phenomenon described is an example of
    A) predation
    B) commensalism
    C) mutualism
    D) parasitism

Life Science 31

18. Which of the following is the type of nonrandom mating that leads to changes in allele frequency?
    A) sexual selection
    B) genetic drift
    C) migration
    D) gene flow

19. Which of the following aquatic biomes are located where freshwater streams empty into the ocean?
    A) wetlands
    B) coral reef
    C) estuaries
    D) littoral

20. Which of the following scenarios accurately describes primary succession?
    A) The ground is scorched by a lava flow; later the establishment of lichens begins on the volcanic rock, leading to the eventual formation of soils.
    B) A meadow is destroyed by a flood; eventually small grasses begin to grow again to begin establishing a healthy meadow ecosystem.
    C) A fire destroys a section of a forest; once the ashes clear, small animals begin making their homes within the area.
    D) A farmer overuses the land causing all the minerals and nutrients in the soil to be used up. Some leftover grass seeds in the soil begin to sprout, repopulating the land.

21. Which of the following organisms generate their own food through photosynthesis and make up the first level of the energy pyramid?
    A) heterotrophs
    B) autotrophs
    C) producers
    D) consumers

22. Which of the following is composed only of members of the same species?
    A) ecosystem
    B) community
    C) biome
    D) population

23. Which of the following type of muscle is responsible for voluntary movement in the body?
    A) cardiac
    B) visceral
    C) smooth
    D) skeletal

24. Which of the following organs is an accessory organ that food does NOT pass through as part of digestion?
    A) pharynx
    B) mouth
    C) small intestine
    D) liver

25. Which of the following is NOT a function of the respiratory system in humans?
    A) to exchange gas
    B) to produce sound and speech
    C) to distribute oxygen to the rest of the body
    D) to remove particles from the air

Answer Key
EXAMPLES

1. **C) is correct.** Amino acid monomers are the building blocks of proteins.

2. **A) is correct.** These are the complementary base pairs that form in DNA.

3. **B) is correct.** Translation is the process of matching codons in RNA to the correct anti-codon to manufacture a protein.

4. **C) is correct.** Ribosomes consist of two subunits built from ribosomal RNA and protein. They are not bound by a membrane.

5. **B) is correct.** The nucleus is the organelle that carries the DNA of eukaryotic organisms.

6. **D) is correct.** The electron transport chain produces thirty to thirty-two molecules of ATP made during cellular respiration. The other choices each produce only two molecules of ATP.

7. **A) is correct.** O_2 is released during the light-dependent stage of photosynthesis and is not used during the Calvin cycle. The other choices are all used during the Calvin cycle to produce glucose.

8. **C) is correct.** The daughter cells produced during mitosis are genetically identical to their diploid (2n) parent.

9. **A) is correct.** This genotype is homozygous, and the recessive trait is the only trait that can be expressed.

10. **C) is correct.** The Punnett square shows that there is a 75 percent chance the child will have the dominant B gene, and thus have brown eyes.

	B	b
B	BB	Bb
b	Bb	bb

11. **D) is correct.** Farmers choosing specific traits in plants is an example of artificial selection.

12. **B) is correct.** Precipitation is a nonliving (abiotic) factor that influences population size.

13. **C) is correct.** Temperate forests have moderate rainfall and are dominated by deciduous trees.

14. **C) is correct.** The alveoli are sacs found at the terminal end of each bronchiole in the lungs and are the site of gas exchange with the blood.

15. **A) is correct.** Most nutrients are absorbed by the small intestine.

TEST YOUR KNOWLEDGE

1. **D) is correct.** Uracil (U) is a pyrimidine found in RNA, replacing the thymine (T) pyrimidine found in DNA.

2. **A) is correct.** Glucose is a monosaccharide that can be used to build larger polysaccharides.

3. **B) is correct.** Translation is process of matching codons in RNA to the correct anti-codon to manufacture a protein.

4. **B) is correct.** Proteins are the expressed products of a gene.

5. **D) is correct.** The cell wall is the structure that gives plant cells their rigidity.

6. **A) is correct.** The smooth endoplasmic reticulum is a series of membranes attached to the cell nucleus and plays an important role in the production and storage of lipids. It is called smooth because it lacks ribosomes on the membrane surface.

7. **A) is correct.** Facilitated diffusion is a form of passive transport across the cell membrane and does not use energy.

8. **B) is correct.** Lactic acid, a byproduct of anaerobic respiration, builds up in muscles and causes fatigue. This occurs when the energy exerted by the muscle exceeds the amount of oxygen available for aerobic respiration.

9. **C) is correct.** Light passes through the epidermis and strikes the pigment chlorophyll, which absorbs the wavelengths of light that humans see as red and blue and reflects the wavelengths of light that the human eye perceives as green.

10. **B) is correct.** Glucose is produced from CO_2 by the energy stored in ATP and the hydrogen atoms associated with NADPH.

11. **B) is correct.** Four haploid (1n) cells are produced during meiosis.

12. **C) is correct.** The Punnett square shows that there is a 75 percent chance the child will have the dominant B gene, and thus have brown eyes.

	B	b
B	BB	Bb
b	Bb	bb

13. **A) is correct.** Because each offspring will inherit the dominant allele, all the offspring will show the dominant phenotype. The offspring would only show a mix of the two phenotypes if they did not follow Mendelian inheritance patterns.

14. **B) is correct.** The offspring has a 50 percent chance of inheriting the dominant allele and a 50 percent chance of inheriting the recessive allele from his mother.

15. **C) is correct.** Type AB blood occurs when two equally dominant alleles (A and B) are inherited. Since they are both dominant, one does not mask the other; instead, both are expressed.

16. **B) is correct.** Competition between species is not necessary for natural selection to occur, although it can influence the traits that are selected for within a population.

17. **B) is correct.** In a commensal relationship, one species benefits with no impact on the other.

18. **A) is correct.** Sexual selection changes allele frequency because it leads to some members of the population reproducing more frequently than others.

19. **C) is correct.** Estuaries are found at the boundary of ocean and stream biomes and are very ecologically productive areas.

20. **A) is correct.** Primary succession can only occur on newly exposed earth that was not previously inhabited by living things. Often this new land is the result of lava flows or glacial movement.

21. **C) is correct.** Producers are a kind of autotroph that are found on the energy pyramid and produce food via photosynthesis.

22. **D) is correct.** A population is all the members of the same species in a given area.

23. **D) is correct.** Skeletal muscles are attached to the skeletal system and are controlled voluntarily.

24. **D) is correct.** The liver is an accessory organ that detoxifies ingested toxins and produces bile for fat digestion.

25. **C) is correct.** The cardiovascular system distributes oxygen to the rest of the body.

CHAPTER THREE
Physical Science

The Structure of the Atom

All matter is composed of very small particles called **ATOMS**. Atom can be further broken down into subatomic particles. **PROTONS**, which are positive, and **NEUTRONS**, which are neutral, form the nucleus of the atom. Negative particles called **ELECTRONS** orbit the nucleus.

While electrons are often depicted as orbiting the nucleus like a planet orbits the sun, they're actually arranged in cloud-like areas called **SHELLS**. The shells closest to the nucleus have the lowest energy and are filled first. The high-energy shells farther from the nucleus only fill with electrons once lower-energy shells are full.

The outermost electron shell of an atom is its **VALENCE SHELL**. The electrons in this shell are involved in chemical reactions. Atoms are most stable when their valence shell is full (usually with eight electrons), so the atom will lose, gain, or share electrons to fill its valence shell.

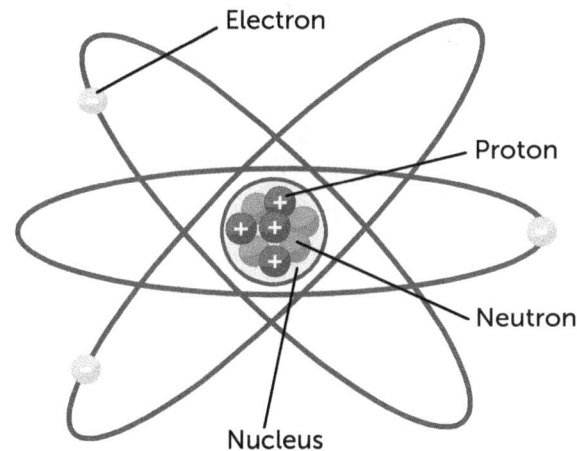

Figure 3.1. Structure of the Atom

A neutral atom will have an equal number of protons and electrons. When a neutral atom loses or gains electrons, it gains or loses charge accordingly, forming an **ION**. An ion with more protons than electrons has a positive charge and is called a **CATION**. An ion with more electrons than protons has a negative charge and is considered an **ANION**.

DID YOU KNOW?
The attractive and repulsive forces in an atom follow the universal law that "like charges repel and opposite charges attract."

For example, the element oxygen (O) has eight protons and eight electrons. A neutral oxygen atom is represented simply as O. However, if it gains two electrons, it becomes an anion with a charge of –2 and is written as O^{2-}.

DID YOU KNOW?
Many element symbols are derived from the Latin names for elements. For example, the Latin name for *gold* is *aurum*, and its symbol is Au.

All atoms with the same number of protons are the same **ELEMENT** and cannot be further reduced to a simpler substance by chemical processes. Each element has a symbol, which is a one- or two-letter abbreviation for the element's name. The number of protons in an atom is that atom's **ATOMIC NUMBER.**

Along with atomic charge, atoms have measurable mass. Protons and neutrons are significantly more massive than electrons (about 1,800 times), so the mass of electrons is not considered when calculating the mass of an atom. Thus, an element's **MASS NUMBER** is the number of protons and neutrons present in its atoms.

EXAMPLES

1. What is the charge of an atom with five protons and seven electrons?
   A) 12
   B) –12
   C) 2
   D) –2

2. Which ion has the greatest number of electrons?
   A) K^+
   B) Cl^-
   C) Ca^+
   D) P^{3-}

The Periodic Table of the Elements

Elements are arranged on the **PERIODIC TABLE OF THE ELEMENTS** by their atomic number, which increases from top to bottom and left to right on the table. Hydrogen, the first element on the periodic table, has one proton while helium, the second element, has two, and so on.

The rows of the periodic table are called **PERIODS**, and the vertical columns are called **GROUPS**. Each group contains elements with the same number of valence electrons, meaning the elements have similar chemical properties.

The majority of the elements in the periodic table are metals. Metals have the following properties:

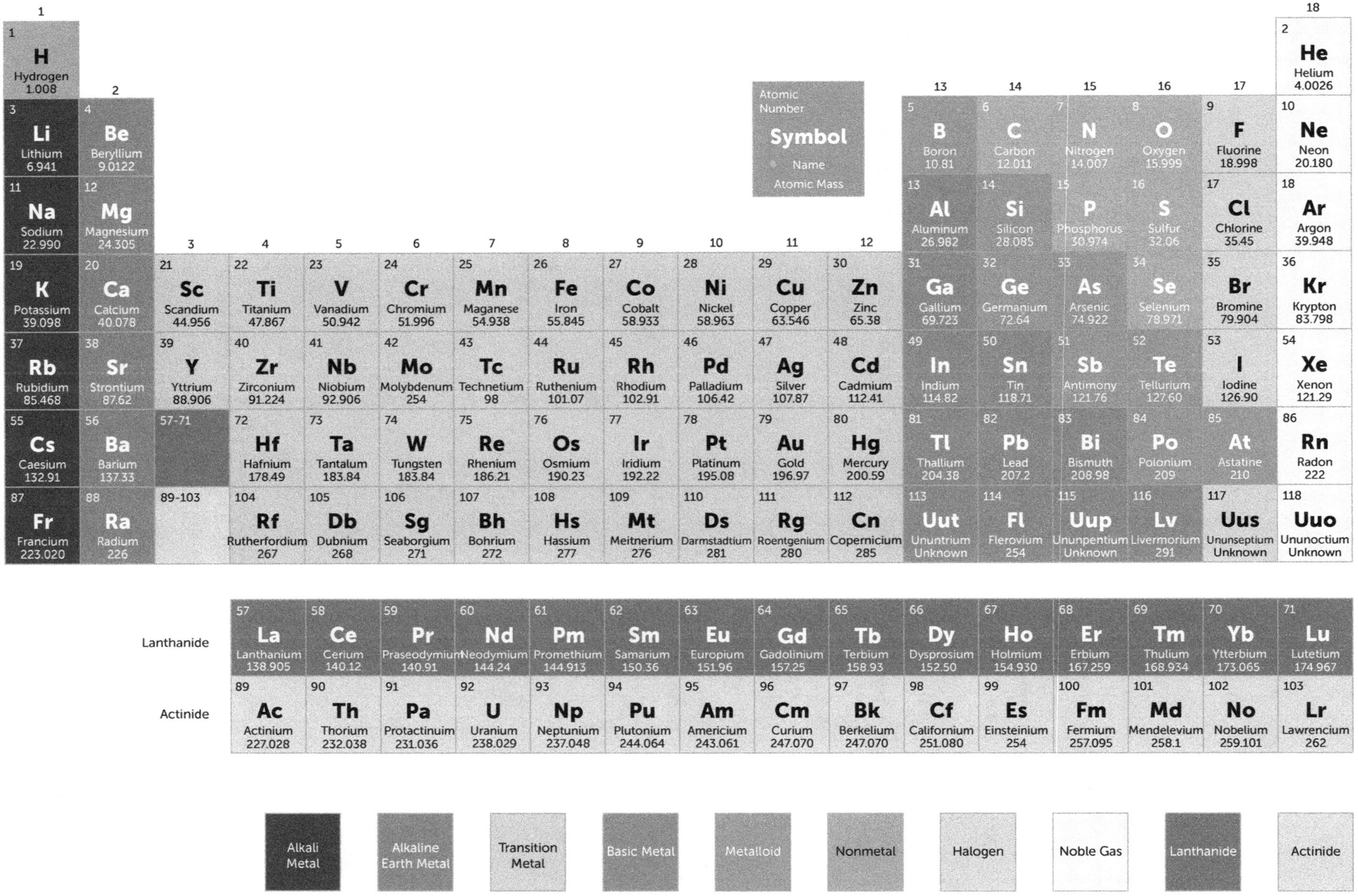

Figure 3.2. Periodic Table

Physical Science 39

- They are hard, opaque, and shiny.
- They are ductile and malleable.
- They conduct electricity and heat.
- With the exception of mercury, they are solids.

METALS begin on the left side of the periodic table and span across the middle of the table, almost all the way to the right side. Examples of metals include gold (Au), tin (Sn), and lead (Pb).

NONMETALS are elements that do not conduct electricity and tend to be more reactive than metals. They can be solids, liquids, or gases. The nonmetals are located on the right side of the periodic table. Examples of nonmetals include sulfur (S), hydrogen (H), and oxygen (O).

METALLOIDS, or semimetals, are elements that possess both metal and nonmetal characteristics. For example, some metalloids are shiny but do not conduct electricity well. Metalloids are located between the metals and nonmetals on the periodic table. Some examples of metalloids are boron (B), silicon (Si), and arsenic (As).

EXAMPLES

3. Bismuth is a
   A) metal.
   B) nonmetal.
   C) metalloid.
   D) transition element.

4. The lithium ion Li⁺ combines with the fluorine ion F⁻ to form the ionic compound LiF. Which of the following elements is fluorine most likely to also form an ionic compound with?
   A) nickel (Ni)
   B) beryllium (Be)
   C) sodium (Na)
   D) argon (Ar)

Chemical Bonds

CHEMICAL BONDS are attractions between atoms that create molecules, which are substances consisting of more than one atom. There are three types of bonds: ionic, covalent, and metallic.

In an **IONIC BOND**, one atom "gives" its electrons to the other, resulting in one positively and one negatively charged atom. The bond is a result of the attraction between the two ions. Ionic bonds form between atoms on the left side of the periodic table (which will lose electrons) and those on the right side (which will gain electrons). Table salt (NaCl) is an example of a molecule held together by an ionic bond.

A **COVALENT BOND** is created by a pair of atoms sharing electrons to fill their valence shells. In a **NONPOLAR** covalent bond, the electrons are shared evenly. In a **POLAR** covalent bond, the electrons are shared unevenly. One atom will exert a stronger pull on the shared electrons, giving that atom a slight negative charge. The other atom in the bond will have a slight positive charge. Water (H_2O) is an example of a polar molecule.

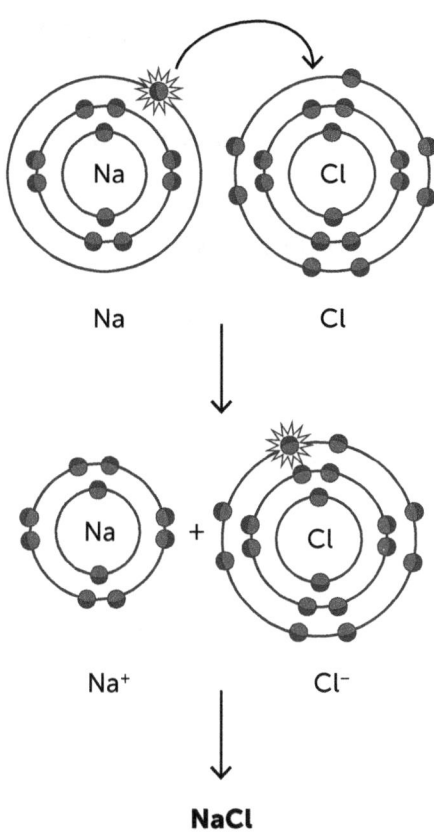

Figure 3.3. The Ionic Bond in Table Salt

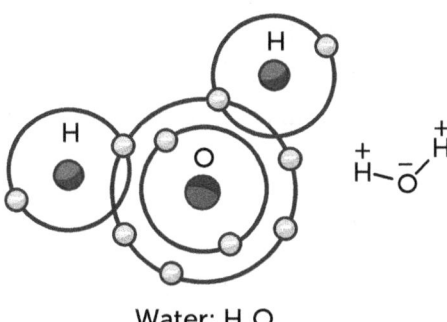

Water: H_2O

Figure 3.4. Polar Covalent Bond

Metals can form tightly packed arrays in which each atom is in close contact with many neighbors. The valence electrons are free to move between atoms and create a "sea" of delocalized charge. Any excitation, such as an electrical current, can cause the electrons to move throughout the array. The high electrical and thermal conductivity of metals is due to this ability of electrons to move throughout the lattice. This type of delocalized bonding is called **METALLIC BONDING**.

DID YOU KNOW?
The polar nature of water is responsible for many of its unique properties. The small charges within a water molecule cause attraction between the molecules. The molecules then "stick" to each other (cohesion) and to other surfaces (adhesion).

EXAMPLE

5. Which of the following compounds is held together by a polar covalent bond?
    A) LiF
    B) CO_2
    C) H_2
    D) NaOH

Physical Science 41

Properties of Matter

MATTER is any substance that takes up space. The amount of matter in an object is that object's **MASS**, which is measured in grams or kilograms. Mass is different from **WEIGHT**, which is a measure of the gravitational force exerted on an object. An object's mass never changes, but its weight will change if the gravitational force changes. The **DENSITY** of an object is the ratio of an object's mass to its volume.

> **DID YOU KNOW?**
> Objects weigh less on the moon than on the earth because the pull of gravity on the moon is lower than that on earth. However, the mass of the object is the same no matter where in the universe it

Properties of substances are divided into two categories: physical and chemical. **PHYSICAL PROPERTIES** are those that are measurable and can be seen without changing the chemical makeup of a substance. In contrast, **CHEMICAL PROPERTIES** are those that determine how a substance will behave in a chemical reaction. Chemical properties cannot be identified simply by observing a material. Instead, the material must be engaged in a chemical reaction in order to identify its chemical properties. A **PHYSICAL CHANGE** is a change in a substance's physical properties, and a **CHEMICAL CHANGE** is a change in its chemical properties.

Table 3.1. Properties of Matter

PHYSICAL PROPERTIES	CHEMICAL PROPERTIES
mass	heat of combustion
temperature	flammability
density	toxicity
color	chemical stability
viscosity	enthalpy of formation

> **DID YOU KNOW?**
> In both physical and chemical changes, matter is always conserved, meaning it can never be created or destroyed.

TEMPERATURE is the name given to the kinetic energy of all the atoms or molecules in a substance. While it might look like matter is not in motion, in fact, its atoms have kinetic energy and are constantly spinning and vibrating. The more energy the atoms have (meaning the more they spin and vibrate) the higher the substance's temperature.

HEAT is the movement of energy from one substance to another. Energy will spontaneously move from high-energy (high-temperature) substances to low-energy (low-temperature) substances.

EXAMPLE

6. Which of the following describes a physical change?
   A) Water becomes ice.
   B) Batter is baked into a cake.
   C) A firecracker explodes.
   D) An acid is neutralized with a base.

States of Matter

All matter exists in different STATES (or phases) that depend on the energy of the molecules in the matter. SOLID matter has densely packed molecules and does not change volume or shape. LIQUIDS have more loosely packed molecules and can change shape but not volume. GAS molecules are widely dispersed, and gases can change both shape and volume.

Changes in temperature and pressure can cause matter to change states. Generally, adding energy (in the form of heat) changes a substance to a higher energy state (e.g., solid to liquid). Transitions from a high to lower energy state (e.g., liquid to solid) release energy. Each of these changes has a specific name, summarized in the table below.

Table 3.2. Changes in State of Matter

Name	From	To	Occurs At	Enery Change
evaporation	liquid	gas	boiling point	uses energy
condensation	gas	liquid	boiling point	releases energy
melting	solid	liquid	freezing point	uses energy
freezing	liquid	solid	freezing point	releases energy
sublimation	solid	gas	---	uses energy
deposition	gas	solid	---	releases energy

EXAMPLE

7. The process that takes place when water reaches its boiling point is called
   A) condensation.
   B) evaporation.
   C) melting.
   D) sublimation.

Physical Science 43

Chemical Reactions

A **CHEMICAL REACTION** occurs when one or more substances react to form new substances. **REACTANTS** are the substances that are consumed or altered in the chemical reaction, and the new substances are **PRODUCTS**. Equations are written with the reactants on the left, the products on the right, and an arrow between them. The state of the chemical compounds are sometimes noted using the labels *s* (solid), *l* (liquid), *g* (gas), or *aq* (aqueous, meaning a solution).

The equation below shows the reaction of hydrogen gas (H_2) and chlorine gas (Cl_2) to form hydrogen chloride (HCl), an acid.

$$H_2\,(g) + Cl_2\,(g) \rightarrow 2HCl\,(aq)$$

Chemical reactions follow the **LAW OF CONSERVATION OF MATTER**, which states that matter cannot be created or destroyed. In a reaction, the same types and numbers of atoms that appear on the left side must also appear on the right. To **BALANCE** a chemical equation, coefficients (the numbers before the reactant or product) are added. In the equation above, a coefficient of two is needed on HCl so that two hydrogen and two chlorine atoms appear on each side of the arrow.

There are five main types of chemical reactions; these are summarized in the table below.

Table 3.3. Types of Reactions		
TYPE OF REACTION	**GENERAL FORMULA**	**EXAMPLE REACTION**
Synthesis	$A + B \rightarrow C$	$2H_2 + O_2 \rightarrow 2H_2O$
Decomposition	$A \rightarrow B + C$	$2H_2O_2 \rightarrow 2H_2O + O_2$
Single displacement	$AB + C \rightarrow A + BC$	$CH_4 + Cl_2 \rightarrow CH_3Cl + HCl$
Double displacement	$AB + CD \rightarrow AC + BD$	$CuCl_2 + 2AgNO_3 \rightarrow Cu(NO_3)_2 + 2AgCl$
Combustion	$C_xH_yO_z + O_2 \rightarrow CO_2 + H_2O$	$2C_8H_{18} + 25O_2 \rightarrow 10CO_2 + 18H_2O$

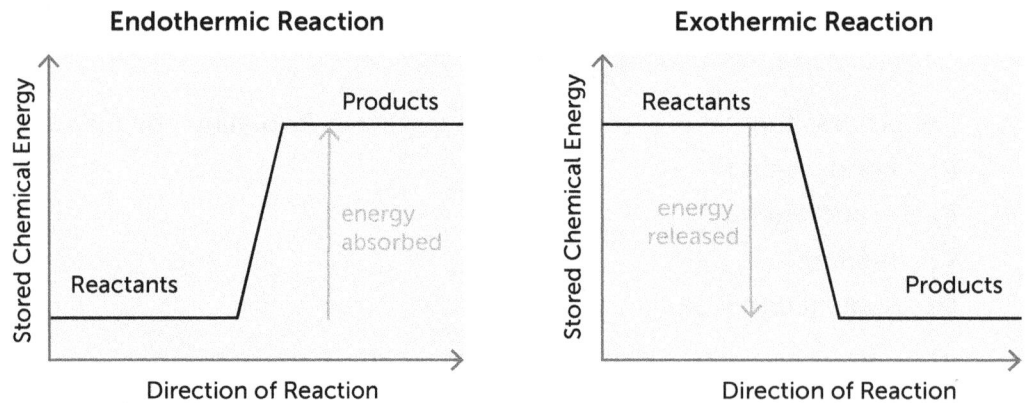

Figure 3.5. Stored Energy in Endothermic and Exothermic Reactions

Energy is required to break chemical bonds, and it is released when bonds form. The total energy absorbed or released during a chemical reaction will depend on the individual bonds being broken and formed. A reaction that releases energy is **EXOTHERMIC**, and a reaction that absorbs energy is **ENDOTHERMIC**.

EXAMPLES

8. Which of the following types of reactions is shown below?
   $Pb(NO_3)_2 + K_2CrO_4 \rightarrow PbCrO_4 + 2KNO_3$
   A) combustion
   B) decomposition
   C) double displacement
   D) single replacement

9. Which of the following equations is a balanced equation?
   A) $2KClO_3 \rightarrow KCl + 3O_2$
   B) $KClO_3 \rightarrow KCl + 3O_2$
   C) $2KClO_3 \rightarrow 2KCl + 3O_2$
   D) $6KClO_3 \rightarrow 6KCl + 3O_2$

Mixtures

When substances are combined without a chemical reaction to bond them, the resulting substance is called a **MIXTURE**. Physical changes can be used to separate mixtures. For example, heating salt water until the water evaporates, leaving the salt behind, will separate a salt water solution.

In a mixture, the components can be unevenly distributed, such as in trail mix or soil. These mixtures are described at **HETEROGENEOUS**. Alternatively, the components can be **HOMOGENEOUSLY**, or uniformly, distributed, as in salt water.

A **SOLUTION** is a special type of stable homogeneous mixture. The components of a solution will not separate on their own and cannot be separated using a filter. The substance being dissolved is the **SOLUTE**, and the substance acting on the solute, or doing the dissolving, is the **SOLVENT**.

The **SOLUBILITY** of a solution is the maximum amount of solute that will dissolve in a specific quantity of solvent at a specified temperature. Solutions can be saturated, unsaturated, or supersaturated based on the amount of solute dissolved in the solution.

▶ A **SATURATED** solution has the maximum amount of solute that can be dissolved in the solvent.

▶ An **UNSATURATED** solution contains less solute than a saturated solution would hold.

DID YOU KNOW?
Solutions can exist as solids, liquids, or gases. For example, carbonated water has a gaseous solute (CO_2) and a liquid solvent (water). A solution formed by combining two solid metals, such as stainless steel, is an **alloy**.

▶ A **SUPERSATURATED SOLUTION** contains more solvent than a saturated solution. A supersaturated solution can be made by heating the solution to dissolve additional solute and then slowly cooling it down to a specified temperature.

EXAMPLES

10. Which of the following is a heterogeneous mixture?
   A) a mixture in which the atoms or molecules are distributed unevenly
   B) a mixture in which two substances are in different states
   C) a mixture of covalent and ionic compounds
   D) a mixture of polar and nonpolar molecules

11. Which of the following terms describes a solution in which more solvent can be dissolved?
   A) unsaturated
   B) saturated
   C) supersaturated
   D) homogeneous

Acids and Bases

Acids and bases are substances that share a distinct set of physical properties. **ACIDS** are corrosive, sour, and change the color of vegetable dyes like litmus from blue to red. **BASES**, or alkaline solutions, are slippery, bitter, and change the color of litmus from red to blue.

DID YOU KNOW?
A **buffer**, or buffer solution, is a solution that resists changes in pH when small quantities of acids or bases are added. A buffer can do this because it contains a weak acid to react with any added base and a weak base to react with any added acid.

There are a number of different ways to define acids and bases, but generally acids release hydrogen ions (H^+) in solution, while bases release hydroxide (OH^-) ions. For example, hydrochloric acid (HCl) ionizes, or breaks apart, in solution to release H^+ ions:

$$HCl \rightarrow H^+ + Cl$$

The base sodium hydroxide (NaOH) ionizes to release OH^- ions:

$$NaOH \rightarrow Na^+ + OH^-$$

Acids and bases combine in a **NEUTRALIZATION REACTION**. During the reaction, the H^+ and OH^- ions join to form water, and the remaining ions combine to form a salt:

$$HCl + NaOH \rightarrow H_2O + NaCl$$

The strength of an acid or base is measured on the **pH SCALE**, which ranges from 1 to 14, with 1 being the strongest acid, 14 being the strongest base, and 7 being neutral.

A substance's pH value is a measure of how many hydrogen ions are in the solution. The scale is logarithmic, meaning an acid with a pH of 3 has ten times as many hydrogen ions as an acid with a pH of 4. Water, which separates into equal numbers of H⁺ and OH⁻ ions, has a neutral pH of 7.

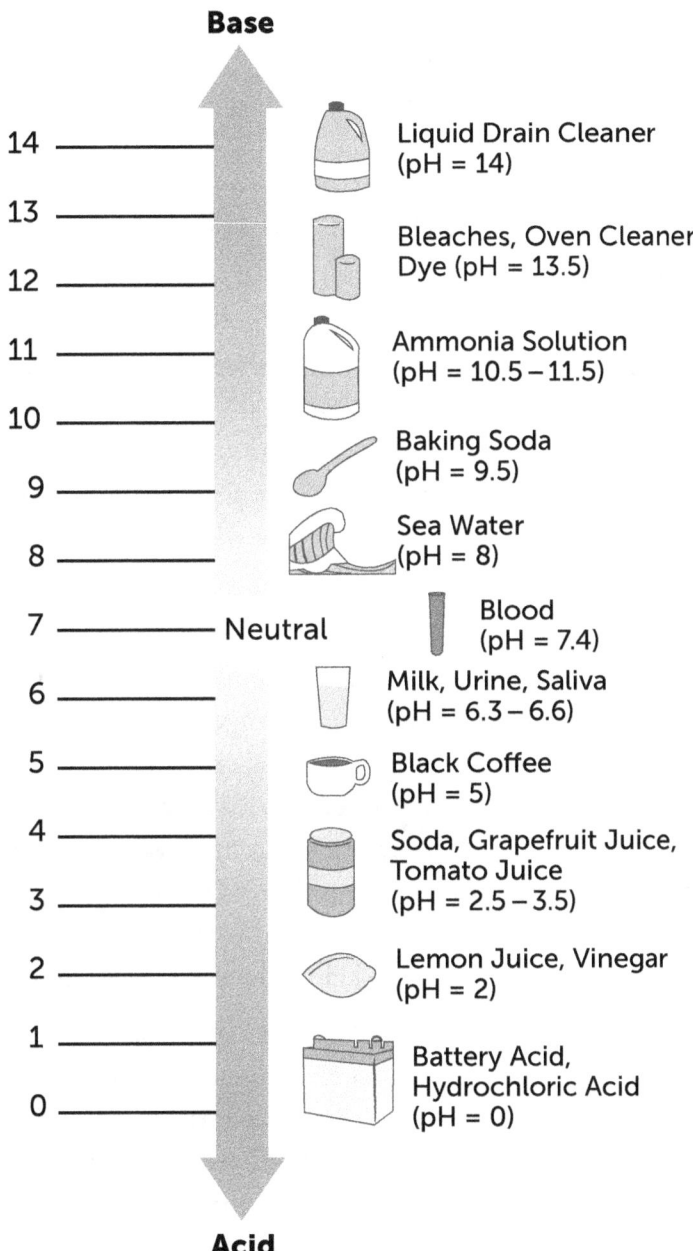

Figure 3.6. The pH Scale

EXAMPLES

12. Which of the following is the product of a neutralization reaction?
   A) a base
   B) a buffer
   C) hydrogen ions
   D) a salt

13. What will happen to the pH of a nitric acid solution that is diluted by a factor of ten?

   A) The pH will go up ten units.
   B) The pH will go down ten units.
   C) The pH will go up one unit.
   D) The pH will go down one unit.

Motion

To study motion, it is necessary to understand the concept of scalars and vectors. **SCALARS** are measurements that have a quantity but no direction. **VECTORS**, in contrast, have both a quantity and a direction. **DISTANCE** is a scalar: it describes how far an object has traveled along a path. Distance can have values such as 54 m or 16 miles. **DISPLACEMENT** is a vector: it describes how far an object has traveled from its starting position. A displacement value will indicate direction, such as 54 m east or –16 miles.

SPEED describes how quickly something is moving. It is found by dividing distance by time, and so is a scalar value. **VELOCITY** is the rate at which an object changes position. Velocity is found by dividing displacement by time, meaning it is a vector value. An object that travels a certain distance and then returns to its starting point has a velocity of zero because its final position did not change. Its speed, however, can be found by dividing the total distance it traveled by the time it took to make the trip.

ACCELERATION describes how quickly an object changes velocity. It is also a vector: when acceleration is in the same direction as velocity, the object will move faster. When the acceleration is in the opposite direction of velocity, the object will slow down.

DID YOU KNOW?
Physical science units include:
mass: kilograms (kg)
displacement: meters (m)
velocity: meters per second (m/s)
acceleration: meters per second per second (m/s^2)
force: Newtons (N)
work: Joules (J)
energy: Joules (J)
current: amperes (A)
voltage: volts (V)

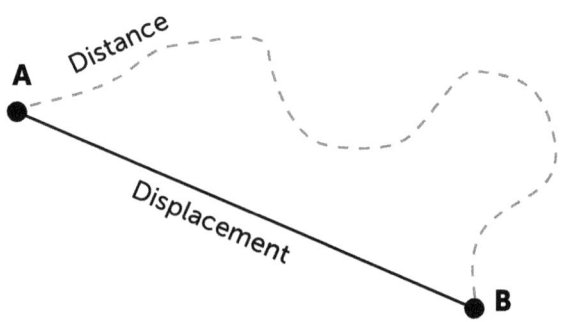

Figure 3.7. Distance versus Displacement

EXAMPLE

14. A person starts from rest and increases his velocity to 5 m/s over a time period of 1 second. What is his acceleration?

    A) –5 m/s^2
    B) 0 m/s^2
    C) 5 m/s^2
    D) 10 m/s^2

Forces

A push or pull that causes an object to move or change direction is called a FORCE. Forces can arise from a number of different sources.

- GRAVITY is the attraction of one mass to another mass. For example, the earth's gravitational field pulls objects toward it, and the sun's gravitational field keeps planets in motion around it.
- ELECTRICAL FORCE is the creation of a field by charged particles that will cause other charged objects in that field to move.
- TENSION is found in ropes pulling or holding up an object.
- FRICTION is created by two objects moving against each other.
- NORMAL FORCE occurs when an object is resting on another object.
- BUOYANT FORCE is the upward force experienced by floating objects.

In 1687, Isaac Newton published THREE LAWS OF MOTION that describe the behavior of force and mass. Newton's first law is also called the LAW OF INERTIA. It states that an object will maintain its current state of motion unless acted on by an outside force.

Newton's SECOND LAW is an equation, $F = ma$. The equation states that increasing the force on an object will increase its acceleration. In addition, the mass of the object will determine its acceleration: under the same force, a small object will accelerate more quickly than a larger object.

An object in equilibrium is either at rest or is moving at constant velocity; in other words, the object has no acceleration, or $a = 0$. Using Newton's second law, an object is in equilibrium if the net force on the object is 0, or $F = 0$ (this is called the equilibrium condition).

Newton's THIRD LAW states that for every action (force), there will be an equal and opposite reaction (force). For instance, if a person is standing on the floor, there is a force of gravity pulling him toward the earth. However, he is not accelerating toward the earth; he is simply standing at rest on the floor (in equilibrium). So, the floor must provide a force that is equal in magnitude and in the opposite direction to the force of gravity.

EXAMPLES

15. When a car moving forward stops abruptly, which of the following describes what happens to the driver if she is wearing a seat belt?
    - A) The driver's body will continue to move forward due to inertia, and the seat belt will apply the required force to keep her in her seat.
    - B) The driver is inside the car, so she will stop with the car whether or not she is wearing a seat belt.
    - C) Due to inertia, the driver's body wants to be at rest, so she will stop automatically once the car stops moving.
    - D) The driver's body will slow down because inertia is passed from the seat belt in the car to the driver.

16. Which example describes an object in equilibrium?
- **A)** a parachutist after he jumps from an airplane
- **B)** an airplane taking off
- **C)** a person sitting still in a chair
- **D)** a soccer ball when it is kicked

Work

Work is a scalar value that is defined as the application of a force over a distance. It is measured in Joules (J).

A person lifting a book off the ground is an example of someone doing work. The book has a weight because it is being pulled toward the earth. As the person lifts the book, her hand and arm are producing a force that is larger than that weight, causing the book to rise. The higher the person lifts the book, the more work is done.

The sign of the work done is important. In the example of lifting a book, the person's hand is doing positive (+) work on the book. However, gravity is always pulling the book down, which means that during a lift, gravity is doing negative (–) work on the book. If the force and the displacement are in the same direction, then the work is positive (+). If the force and the displacement are in opposite directions, then the work is negative (–). In the case of lifting a book, the net work done on the book is positive.

EXAMPLE

17. Which situation requires the most work done on a car?
- **A)** pushing on the car, but it does not move
- **B)** towing the car up a steep hill for 100 meters
- **C)** pushing the car 5 meters across a parking lot
- **D)** painting the car

Energy

Energy is an abstract concept, but everything in nature has an energy associated with it. Energy is measured in Joules (J). There are many types of energy:

- mechanical: the energy of motion
- chemical: the energy in chemical bonds
- thermal: the energy of an object due to its temperature
- nuclear: the energy in the nucleus of an atom
- electric: the energy arising from charged particles
- magnetic: the energy arising from a magnetic field

There is an energy related to movement called the KINETIC ENERGY (KE). Any object that has mass and is moving will have a kinetic energy.

POTENTIAL ENERGY (PE) is the energy stored in a system; it can be understood as the potential for an object to gain kinetic energy. There are several types of potential energy.

- ELECTRIC POTENTIAL ENERGY is derived from the interaction between positive and negative charges.
- Compressing a spring stores ELASTIC POTENTIAL ENERGY.
- Energy is also stored in chemical bonds as CHEMICAL POTENTIAL ENERGY.
- The energy stored by objects due to their height is GRAVITATIONAL POTENTIAL ENERGY.

Energy can be converted into other forms of energy, but it cannot be created or destroyed. This principle is called the CONSERVATION OF ENERGY. A swing provides a simple example of this principle. Throughout the swing's path, the total energy of the system remains the same. At the highest point of a swing's path, it has potential energy but no kinetic energy (because it has stopped moving momentarily as it changes direction). As the swing drops, that potential energy is converted to kinetic energy, and the swing's velocity increases. At the bottom of its path, all its potential energy has been converted into kinetic energy (meaning its potential energy is zero). This process repeats as the swing moves up and down. At any point in the swing's path, the kinetic and potential energies will sum to the same value.

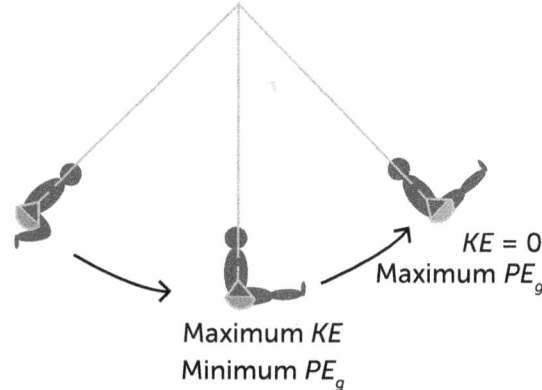

Figure 3.8. Conservation of Energy in a Swing

EXAMPLES

18. Imagine a roller coaster that does not have its own power and starts on a hill at a height of 100 meters. There is no air resistance or friction. It falls down to a height of 50 meters in the first dip and begins to move up the next hill, which is 200 meters high. What will happen to the coaster on this hill?

    A) It will slow down but will make it over the 200 meter hill.
    B) It will make it 150 meters up the hill and move back down to the first dip.
    C) It will make it 100 meters up the hill and move back down to the first dip.
    D) It will make it 75 meters up the hill and move back down to the first dip.

Physical Science

19. A pendulum with mass *m* is swinging back and forth. Which of the following statements about the pendulum's speed is true?

- **A)** The maximum speed of the mass will occur when it's closest to the ground.
- **B)** The maximum speed of the mass will occur when it's farthest from the ground.
- **C)** The mass will always travel at the same speed.
- **D)** The maximum speed of the mass will occur when it is halfway between its lowest and highest point.

Waves

Energy can also be transferred through **WAVES**, which are repeating pulses of energy. Waves that travel through a medium, like ripples on a pond or compressions in a Slinky, are called **MECHANICAL WAVES**. Waves that vibrate up and down (like the ripples on a pond) are **TRANSVERSE WAVES**, and those that travel through compression (like the Slinky) are **LONGITUDINAL WAVES**. Mechanical waves will travel faster through denser mediums; for example, sound waves will move faster through water than through air.

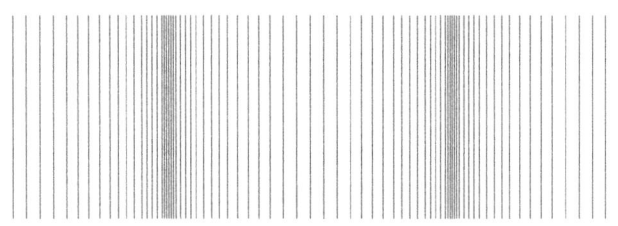

Longitudinal Wave

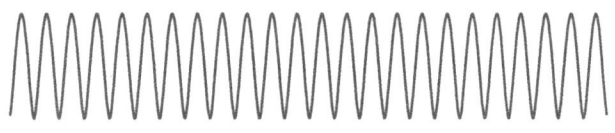

Transverse Wave

Figure 3.9. Types of Waves

Waves can be described using a number of different properties. A wave's highest point is called its **CREST**, and its lowest point is the **TROUGH**. A wave's **MIDLINE** is halfway between the crest and trough; the **AMPLITUDE** describes the distance between the midline and the crest (or trough). The distance between crests (or troughs) is the **WAVELENGTH**. A wave's **PERIOD** is the time it takes for a wave to go through one complete cycle, and the number of cycles a wave goes through in a specific period of time is its **FREQUENCY**.

SOUND is a special type of longitudinal wave created by vibrations. Our ears are able to interpret these waves as particular sounds. The frequency, or rate, of the vibration determines the sound's **PITCH**. **LOUDNESS** depends on the amplitude, or height, of a sound wave.

The **DOPPLER EFFECT** is the difference in perceived pitch caused by the motion of the object creating the wave. For example, as an ambulance approaches an observer, the siren's pitch will appear to increase, and then as the ambulance moves away, the siren's pitch will appear to decrease. This occurs because sound waves are compressed as the ambulance approaches the observer and are spread out as the ambulance moves away from the observer.

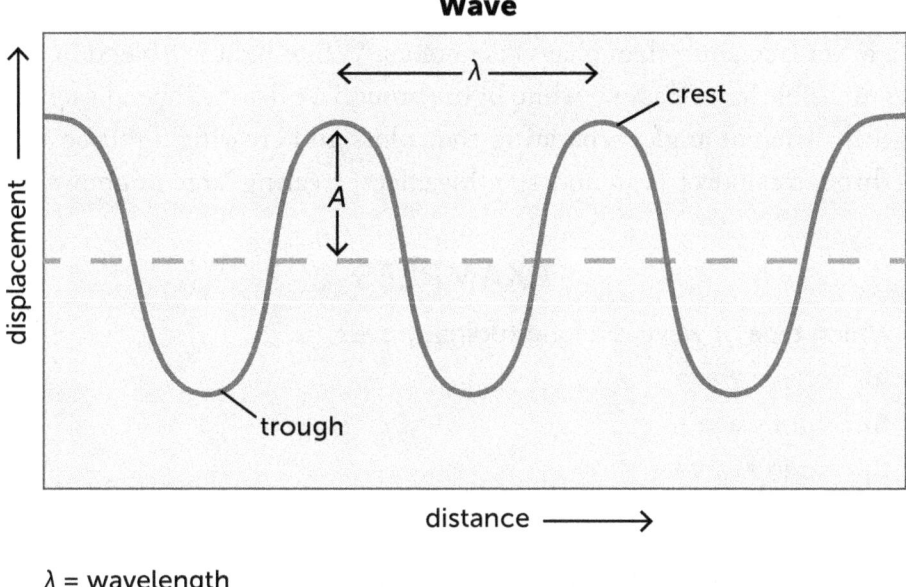

Figure 3.10. Parts of a Wave

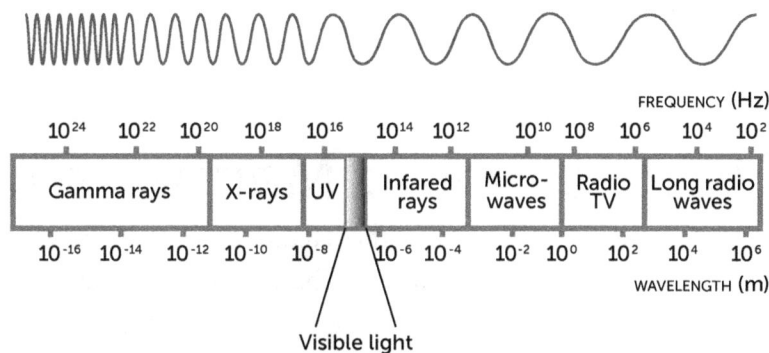

Figure 3.11. The Electromagnetic Spectrum

ELECTROMAGNETIC WAVES are composed of oscillating electric and magnetic fields and thus do not require a medium through which to travel. The electromagnetic spectrum classifies the types of electromagnetic waves based on their frequency. These include radio waves, microwaves, X-rays, and visible light.

The study of light is called **OPTICS**. Because visible light is a wave, it will display properties that are similar to other waves. It will **REFLECT**, or bounce off, surfaces, which can be observed by shining a flashlight on a mirror. Light will also **REFRACT**, or bend, when it travels between substances. This effect can be seen by placing a pencil in water and observing the apparent bend in the pencil.

Curved pieces of glass called **LENSES** can be used to bend light in a way that affects how an image is perceived. Some microscopes, for example, make objects appear larger through the use of specific types of lenses. Eyeglasses also use lenses to correct poor vision.

The frequency of a light wave is responsible for its color, with red/orange colors having a lower frequency than blue/violet colors. White light is a blend of all the frequencies of visible light. Passing white light through a prism will bend each frequency at a slightly different angle, separating the colors and creating a rainbow. Sunlight passing through raindrops can undergo this effect, creating large rainbows in the sky.

EXAMPLES

20. Which type of wave is a longitudinal wave?
- **A)** ocean wave
- **B)** light wave
- **C)** sound wave
- **D)** X-ray wave

21. Which of the following events is caused by refraction?
- **A)** a rainbow during a rainstorm
- **B)** an echo in a cave
- **C)** a candle appearing in a mirror
- **D)** the Doppler effect

Electricity and Magnetism

ELECTRIC CHARGE is created by a difference in the balance of protons and electrons, which creates a positively or negatively charged object. Charged objects create an **ELECTRIC FIELD** that spreads outward from the object. Other charged objects in that field will experience a force: objects that have opposite charges will be attracted to each other, and objects with the same charge will be repelled, or pushed away, from each other.

Because protons cannot leave the nucleus, charge is created by the movement of electrons. **STATIC ELECTRICITY**, or electrostatic charge, occurs when a surface has a buildup of charges. For example, if a student rubs a balloon on her head, the friction will cause electrons to move from her hair to the balloon. This creates a negative charge on the balloon and a positive charge on her hair; the resulting attraction will cause her hair to move toward the balloon.

ELECTRICITY is the movement of electrons through a conductor, and an electric circuit is a closed loop through which electricity moves. Circuits include a **VOLTAGE** source, which powers the movement of electrons known as **CURRENT**. Sources of voltage include batteries, generators, and wall outlets (which are in turn powered by electric power stations). Other elements, such as lights, computers, and microwaves, can then be connected to the circuit and then powered by its electricity.

Magnets are created by the alignment of spinning electrons within a substance. This alignment will occur naturally in some substances, including iron, nickel, and cobalt, all of which can be used to produce permanent magnets. The alignment of electrons creates a magnetic field, which, like an electric or gravitational field, can act on other objects. Magnetic fields have a north and a south pole that act similarly to electric charges: opposite poles will attract, and same poles will repel each other. However, unlike electric charge, which can be either positive or negative, a magnetic field ALWAYS has two poles. If a magnet is cut in half, the result is two magnets, each with a north and a south pole.

Electricity and magnetism are closely related. A moving magnet creates an electric field, and a moving charged particle creates a magnetic field. A specific kind of temporary magnet known as an **ELECTROMAGNET** can be made by coiling a wire around a metal object and running electricity through it. A magnetic field will be created when the wire contains a current but will disappear when the flow of electricity is stopped.

EXAMPLES

22. What part of the atom flows through a circuit to power a light bulb?
    A) protons
    B) neutrons
    C) electrons
    D) nucleus

23. Which metal attracts magnets?
    A) iron
    B) copper
    C) silver
    D) gold

Test Your Knowledge

Read the question, and then choose the most correct answer.

1. Which of the following determines the atomic number of an atom?
   A) the number of electrons orbiting the nucleus
   B) the number of protons in the nucleus
   C) the number of protons and neutrons in the nucleus
   D) the number of protons and electrons in the atom

2. How many neutrons are in an atom of the element $^{88}_{38}Sr$?
   A) 38
   B) 88
   C) 50
   D) 126

3. Refer to the periodic table in Figure 3.2. Which element is a metalloid?
   A) rubidium
   B) vanadium
   C) antimony
   D) iodine

4. Which of the following is NOT a typical property of metals?
   A) Metals have low densities.
   B) Metals are malleable.
   C) Metals are good conductors of electricity and heat.
   D) Metals in solid state consist of ordered structures with tightly packed atoms.

5. Which element has chemical properties most similar to sulfur?
   A) fluorine
   B) argon
   C) phosphorus
   D) oxygen

6. Which of the following groups on the periodic table will typically adopt a charge of +1 when forming ionic compounds?
   A) alkaline earth metals
   B) lanthanides
   C) actinides
   D) alkali metals

7. Match the elements with the type of bond that would occur between them.

Elements	Bond
magnesium and bromine	
carbon and oxygen	
solid copper	

   A) ionic
   B) metallic
   C) covalent

8. Label each compound as polar or nonpolar.

Compound	Polar	Nonpolar
H_2O		
F_2		
HF		

9. How many electrons are included in the double bond between the two oxygen atoms in O_2?
   A) 2
   B) 4
   C) 6
   D) 8

10. Which of the following describes a physical change?
    A) Water becomes ice.
    B) Batter is baked into a cake.
    C) An iron fence rusts.
    D) A firecracker explodes.

11. Which of the following processes produces a gas from a solid?
    A) melting
    B) evaporation
    C) condensation
    D) sublimation

12. Which of the following is a double replacement reaction?
    A) HNO_3 (aq) + NaOH (aq) → $NaNO_3$ (aq) + H_2O (l)
    B) CS_2 (g) + CO_2 (g) → 2COS (g)
    C) $2N_2O$ (g) → $2N_2$ (g) + O_2 (g)
    D) $BaCl_2$ (aq) + H_2SO_4 (aq) → 2HCl (aq) + $BaSO_4$ (s)

13. Balance the following chemical equation:
    $P_4 + O_2 + H_2O → H_3PO_4$
    A) 1:8:6:4
    B) 1:2:2:4
    C) 1:2:6:4
    D) 1:5:6:4

14. Which of the following is NOT a homogeneous mixture?
    A) air
    B) sandy water
    C) brass
    D) salt dissolved in water

15. Which trait defines a saturated solution?
    A) Both the solute and solvent are liquid.
    B) The solute is distributed evenly throughout the solution.
    C) The solute is unevenly distributed throughout the solution.
    D) No more solute can be dissolved in the solution.

16. Which of the following is NOT a definition of an acid?
    A) A substance that contains hydrogen and produces H⁺ in water.
    B) A substance that donates protons to a base.
    C) A substance that reacts with a base to form a salt and water.
    D) A substance that accepts protons.

17. A ball is tossed straight into the air with a velocity of 3 m/s. What will its velocity be at its maximum height?
    A) −3 m/s
    B) 0 m/s
    C) 1.5 m/s
    D) 3 m/s

18. How far will a car moving at 40 m/s travel in 2 seconds?
    A) 10 m
    B) 20 m
    C) 40 m
    D) 80 m

19. If a baseball thrown straight up in the air takes 5 seconds to reach its peak, how long will it need to fall back to the player's hand?
    A) 2.5 seconds
    B) 9.8 seconds
    C) 5.0 seconds
    D) 10.0 seconds

20. Which of the following is a measure of the inertia of an object?
    A) mass
    B) speed
    C) acceleration
    D) force

21. A box sliding down a ramp experiences all of the following forces EXCEPT
    A) tension.
    B) friction.
    C) gravitational.
    D) normal.

22. A person with a mass of 80 kg travels to the moon, where the acceleration due to gravity is 1.62 m/s². What will her mass be on the moon?
    A) greater than 80 kg
    B) 80 kg
    C) less than 80 kg
    D) The answer cannot be determined without more information.

23. If a force of 300 N is pushing on a block to the right and a force of 400 N is pushing on a block to the left, what is the net force on the block?
    A) 0 N
    B) 100 N to the left
    C) 300 N to the right
    D) 400 N to the left

24. A man is pushing against a heavy rock sitting on a flat plane, and the rock is not moving. The force that holds the rock in place is
    A) friction.
    B) gravity.
    C) normal force.
    D) buoyant force.

25. Which of the following describes what will happen when positive work is done on an object?
    A) The object will gain energy.
    B) The object will lose energy.
    C) The object will increase its temperature.
    D) The object will decrease its temperature.

26. What type of energy is stored in the bond between hydrogen and oxygen in water (H_2O)?
    A) mechanical
    B) chemical
    C) nuclear
    D) electric

27. A microscope makes use of which property of waves to make objects appear larger?
    A) diffraction
    B) amplitude
    C) reflection
    D) refraction

28. Which measurement describes the distance between crests in a wave?

A) amplitude
B) wavelength
C) frequency
D) period

29. Two negative charges are being held 1 meter apart. What will the charges do when they are released?

A) They will move closer together.
B) They will move farther apart.
C) They will stay 1 meter apart and move in the same direction.
D) They will stay 1 meter apart and not move.

30. The north poles of two magnets are held near each other. At which distance will the magnets experience the most force?

A) 0.1 meters
B) 1 meters
C) 10 meters
D) 100 meters

Physical Science

Answer Key
EXAMPLES

1. **D) is correct.** The total charge of an atom is the difference between the number of protons and electrons. Subtract the number of electrons from the number of protons: 5 − 7 = −2.

2. **C) is correct.** Calcium has an atomic number of 20 (found on the Periodic table), meaning it has 20 protons. For a Ca ion to have a charge of 1+, it must have nineteen electrons. All the other ions have eighteen electrons.

3. **A) is correct.** Bismuth is a metal.

4. **C) is correct.** Lithium and sodium are both in Group 1 of the periodic table, so they have similar chemical properties. Sodium will form the ion Na^+ and join with F^- to form NaF.

5. **B) is correct.** Carbon and oxygen are both nonmetals that combine through a covalent bond. Oxygen has a strong pull on their shared electrons, so CO_2 is polar. In hydrogen gas (H_2), the identical hydrogen atoms share electrons equally, so the compound is nonpolar. Choices A) and D) are ionic compounds.

6. **A) is correct.** When water changes form, it does not change the chemical composition of the substance. Once water becomes ice, the ice can easily turn back into water by increasing its temperature.

7. **B) is correct.** Evaporation is the process of conversion from liquid to gas that occurs at the boiling point.

8. **C) is correct.** In the reaction, the Pb and K exchange their anions in a double-displacement reaction.

9. **C) is correct.** In this equation, there are equal numbers of each type of atom on both sides (2 K atoms, 2 Cl atoms, and 6 O atoms).

10. **A) is correct.** A heterogeneous mixture is any non-uniform mixture, which means that the atoms or molecules are unevenly distributed.

11. **A) is correct.** An unsaturated solution has less solute than can be dissolved in the given amount of solvent.

12. **D) is correct.** A neutralization reaction occurs when an acid and a base combine to form a salt and water.

13. **C) is correct.** The pH will go up: diluting an acid will decrease the concentration of H^+ ions, and higher pH values represent lower concentrations of H^+ ions. Diluting the acid by a factor of ten will change the pH one unit because the pH scale is logarithmic.

14. **C) is correct.** Acceleration is the change in velocity over the change in time:
$$a = \frac{v}{t} = \frac{(5 \text{ m/s} - 0 \text{ m/s})}{1 \text{ s}} = \mathbf{5 \text{ m/s}^2}$$

15. A) is correct. The driver's body will continue moving forward due to inertia. A force is required to slow the driver down (Newton's first law).

16. C) is correct. A person sitting in a chair is not accelerating. All the other choices describe objects that are accelerating, or changing velocity.

17. B) is correct. A steep hill requires a large force to counter the gravitational force. The large distance will also lead to a large amount of work done. Less work is done in choice C), and no work is done in choice A). Choice D) is incorrect because painting the car is "work," but not the technical definition of work. The car is not moving while being painted, so no work is done on the car.

18. C) is correct. Its maximum energy is from its starting point, the potential energy at 100 meters, so it can never move higher than 100 meters.

19. A) is correct. The mass always has the same total energy. When the height is the lowest, the potential energy is at its minimum, and so the kinetic energy is at its maximum. When kinetic energy is high, the mass's velocity will be at its height.

20. C) is correct. Sound waves are longitudinal waves because the vibrations travel in the same direction as the energy.

21. A) is correct. The light of the sun hits rain droplets and bends into a band of colors. The bending of waves is refraction.

22. C) is correct. Electrons are negatively charged subatomic particles that exist outside the nucleus of an atom. A power source forces moving electrons through a circuit.

23. A) is correct. Magnets readily attract iron. The other metals are not attracted to magnets.

TEST YOUR KNOWLEDGE

1. **B) is correct.** Atomic number is defined as the total number of protons in the nucleus of an atom.

2. **C) is correct.** Subtracting the atomic number from the mass number gives the number of protons: $A - Z = 88 - 38 = 50$.

3. **C) is correct.** Antimony is a metalloid. Rubidium is a metal, vanadium is a transition metal, and iodine is a halogen.

4. **A) is correct.** Because metals tend to consist of ordered, tightly packed atoms, their densities are typically high (not low).

5. **D) is correct.** Oxygen is in the same group as sulfur and is also a nonmetal.

6. **D) is correct.** By losing one electron and thereby adopting a +1 charge, alkali metals achieve a noble gas electron configuration, making them more stable.

7.

Elements	Bond
magnesium and bromine	**A) is correct.** Ionic bonds form between elements on the left side of the periodic table and the right side.
carbon and oxygen	**C) is correct.** Nonmetals tend to form covalent bonds.
solid copper	**B) is correct.** Solid metals are held together by metallic bonding.

8.

Compound	Polar	Nonpolar
H_2O	O attracts electrons more strongly than H, and H_2O is bent such that the charges on each O do not balance.	
F_2		Because the two atoms are the same, they share electrons equally.
HF	F attracts electrons more strongly than H, creating a polar molecule.	

9. **B) is correct.** The two oxygen atoms in a covalent double bond share two pairs of electrons, or four total.

10. **A) is correct.** When water changes form, it does not change the chemical composition of the substance. Once water becomes ice, the ice can easily turn back into water.

11. **D) is correct.** Sublimation is the phase change in which a material moves directly from the solid phase to the gas phase, bypassing the liquid phase.

12. **D) is correct.** This reaction is a double replacement reaction in which the two reactants change partners. Ba^{+2} combines with SO_4^{-2} and H^{+1} combines with Cl^{-1}.

13. **D) is correct.**

    $\_P_4 + \_O_2 + \_H_2O \rightarrow \_H_3PO_4$

    Add a 4 on the right side to balance the four P atoms on the left.

    $\_P_4 + \_O_2 + \_H_2O \rightarrow 4H_3PO_4$

    There are now twelve H atoms on the right, so add a 6 to H_2O on the left.

    $\_P_4 + \_O_2 + 6H_2O \rightarrow 4H_3PO_4$

    There are sixteen O on the right, so add a 5 to O_2 on the left.

    $P_4 + 5O_2 + 6H_2O \rightarrow 4H_3PO_4$

14. **B) is correct.** Sandy water is not a homogeneous mixture. Sand and water can be easily separated, making it a heterogeneous mixture.

15. **D) is correct.** No more solute can be dissolved into a saturated solution.

16. **D) is correct.** Acids increase the concentration of hydrogen ions in solution and do not accept protons.

17. **B) is correct.** The velocity of a projectile is zero at its maximum height.

18. **D) is correct.** Displacement is equal to velocity multiplied by time:

    $d = vt = (40 \text{ m/s})(2 \text{ s}) = $ **80 m**

19. **C) is correct.** The time to the peak and the time to fall back to the original height are equal.

20. **A) is correct.** Mass is a measure of an object's inertia.

21. **A) is correct.** Tension is the force that results from objects being pulled or hung.

22. **B) is correct.** The mass of an object is constant, so the mass would still be 80 kg. (However, the person's weight would be lower on the moon than on the earth.)

23. **B) is correct.** The total force on an object is found by adding all the individual forces: 300 N + (−400 N) = −100 N (where negative is to the left).

24. **A) is correct.** When the man pushes on the rock, static friction points opposite the direction of the applied force with the same magnitude. The forces add to zero, so the rock's acceleration is also zero.

25. **A) is correct.** The object will gain energy.

26. **B) is correct.** Chemical energy is stored in the bonds between atoms.

Physical Science

27. D) is correct. Lenses refract, or bend, light waves to make objects appear larger.

28. B) is correct. Wavelength is the length of each cycle of the wave, which can be found by measuring between crests.

29. B) is correct. Like charges repel each other, so the two charges will move apart from each other.

30. A) is correct. Magnetic force is inversely proportional to the distance between two objects, so the smallest distance will create the largest force.

CHAPTER FOUR
Earth and Space Science

Astronomy

Astronomy is the study of space. Our planet, **Earth**, is just one out of a group of planets that orbit the sun, which is the star at the center of our solar system. Other planets in our solar system include Mercury, Venus, Mars, Jupiter, Saturn, Uranus, and Neptune.

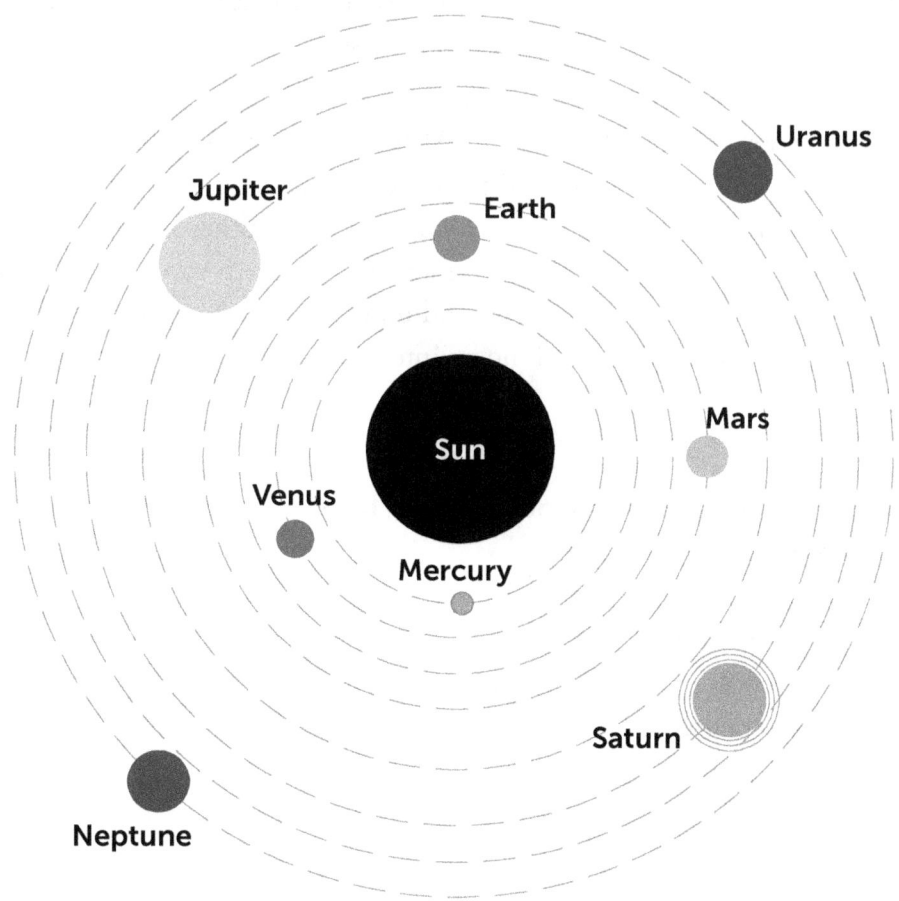

Figure 4.1. Solar System

Every planet, except Mercury and Venus, has **MOONS**, or naturally occurring satellites that orbit a planet. Our solar system also includes **ASTEROIDS** and **COMETS**, small rocky or icy objects that orbit the Sun. Many of these are clustered in the **ASTEROID BELT**, which is located between the orbits of Mars and Jupiter.

Our solar system is a small part of a bigger star system called a **GALAXY**. (Our galaxy is called the Milky Way.) Galaxies consist of stars, gas, and dust held together by gravity and contain millions of **STARS**, which are hot balls of plasma and gases. The universe includes many types of stars, including supergiant stars, white dwarfs, giant stars, and neutron stars. Stars form in **NEBULAS**, which are large clouds of dust and gas. When very large stars collapse, they create **BLACK HOLES**, which have a gravitational force so strong that light cannot escape.

Earth, the moon, and the sun interact in a number of ways that impact life on our planet. When the positions of the three align, eclipses occur. A **LUNAR ECLIPSE** occurs when Earth lines up between the moon and the sun; the moon moves into the shadow of Earth and appears dark in color. A **SOLAR ECLIPSE** occurs when the moon lines up between Earth and the sun; the moon covers the sun, blocking sunlight.

The cycle of day and night and the seasonal cycle are determined by the earth's motion. It takes approximately 365 days, or one **YEAR**, for Earth to revolve around the sun. While Earth is revolving around the sun, it is also rotating on its axis, which takes approximately twenty-four hours, or one **DAY**. As the planet rotates, different areas alternately face toward the sun and away from the sun, creating night and day.

The earth's axis is not directly perpendicular to its orbit, meaning the planet tilts on its axis. The **SEASONS** are caused by this tilt. When the Northern Hemisphere is tilted toward the sun, it receives more sunlight and experiences summer. At the same time that the Northern Hemisphere experiences summer, the Southern Hemisphere, which receives less direct sunlight, experiences winter. As the earth revolves, the Northern Hemisphere will tilt away from the sun and move into winter, while the Southern Hemisphere tilts toward the sun and moves into summer.

EXAMPLE

1. What term describes what occurs when the moon moves between the earth and the sun?
   A) aurora
   B) lunar eclipse
   C) black hole
   D) solar eclipse

Geology

GEOLOGY is the study of the minerals and rocks that make up the earth. A **MINERAL** is a naturally occurring, solid, inorganic substance with a crystalline structure. There are several properties that help identify a mineral, including color, luster, hardness, and density. Examples of minerals include talc, diamonds, and topaz.

Although a **ROCK** is also a naturally occurring solid, it can be either organic or inorganic and is composed of one or more minerals. Rocks are classified based on their method of formation. The three types of rocks are igneous, sedimentary, and metamorphic. **IGNEOUS ROCKS** are the result of tectonic processes that bring magma, or melted rock, to the earth's surface; they can form either above or below the surface. **SEDIMENTARY ROCKS** are formed from the compaction of rock fragments that results from weathering and erosion. Lastly, **METAMORPHIC ROCKS** form when extreme temperature and pressure cause the structure of pre-existing rocks to change.

DID YOU KNOW?
Luster describes how light reflects off the surface of a mineral. Terms to describe luster include dull, metallic, pearly, and waxy.

The **ROCK CYCLE** describes how rocks form and break down. Typically, the cooling and solidification of magma as it rises to the surface creates igneous rocks. These rocks are then subject to **WEATHERING**, the mechanical and/or chemical processes by which rocks break down. During **EROSION** the resulting sediment is deposited in a new location. As sediment is deposited, the resulting compaction creates new sedimentary rocks. As new layers are added, rocks and minerals are forced closer to the earth's core where they are subjected to heat and pressure, resulting in metamorphic rock. Eventually, they will reach their melting point and return to magma, starting the cycle over again. This process takes place over hundreds of thousands or even millions of years.

PALEONTOLOGY, the study of the history of life on Earth, is sometimes also considered part of geology. Paleontologists study the rock record, which retains biological history through **FOSSILS**, the preserved remains and traces of ancient life. Fossils can be used to

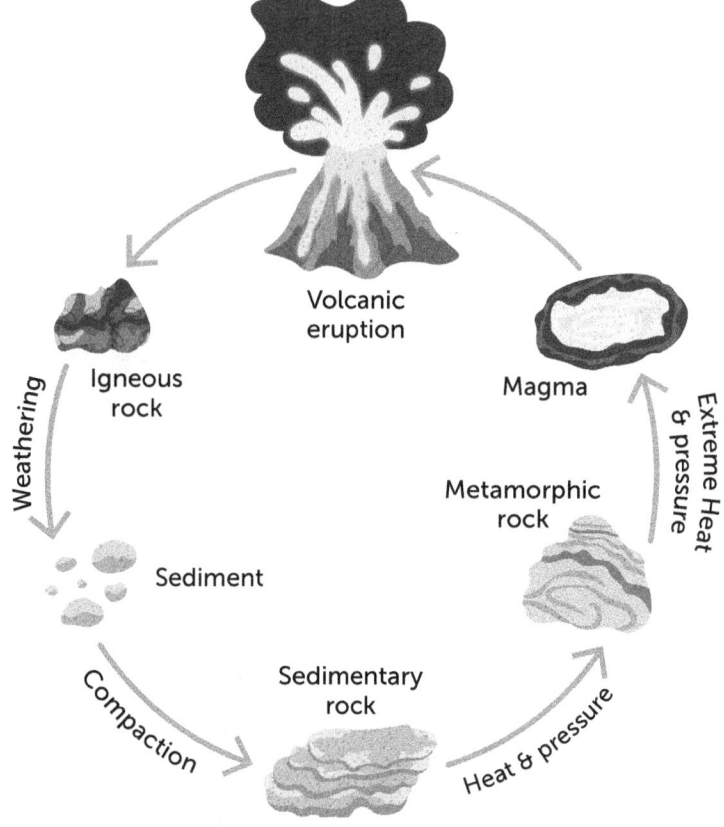

Figure 4.2. The Rock Cycle

Earth and Space Science

learn about the evolution of life on the planet, particularly bacteria, plants, and animals that have gone extinct. Throughout Earth's history, there have been five documented catastrophic events that caused major extinctions. For each mass extinction, there are several theories about the cause but no definitive answers. Theories about what triggered mass extinctions include climate change, ice ages, asteroid and comet impacts, and volcanic activity.

The surface of the earth is made of large plates that float on the less dense layer beneath them. These **TECTONIC PLATES** make up the lithosphere, the planet's surface layer. Over 200 million years ago, the continents were joined together in one giant landmass called **PANGEA**. Due to **CONTINENTAL DRIFT**, or the slow movement of tectonic plates, the continents gradually shifted to their current positions.

DID YOU KNOW?
The magnitude of an earthquake refers to the amount of energy it releases, measured as the maximum motion during the earthquake. This can indirectly describe how destructive the earthquake was.

The boundaries where plates meet are the locations for many geologic features and events. **MOUNTAINS** are formed when plates collide and push land upward, and **TRENCHES** form when one plate is pushed beneath another. In addition, the friction created by plates sliding past each other is responsible for most **EARTHQUAKES**.

VOLCANOES, which are vents in the earth's crust that allow molten rock to reach the surface, frequently occur along the edges of tectonic plates. However, they can also occur at hotspots located far from plate boundaries.

The outermost layer of the earth, which includes tectonic plates, is called the **LITHOSPHERE**. Beneath the lithosphere are, in order, the **ASTHENOSPHERE**, **MESOSPHERE**, and **CORE**. The core includes two parts: the **OUTER CORE** is a liquid layer, and the **INNER CORE** is composed of solid iron. It is believed the inner core spins at a rate slightly different from the rest of the planet, which creates the earth's magnetic field.

EXAMPLE

2. Which type of rock forms when lava cools and solidifies?
   A) igneous
   B) sedimentary
   C) metamorphic
   D) sandstone

Hydrology

The earth's surface includes many bodies of water that together form the **HYDROSPHERE**. The largest of these are the bodies of salt water called **OCEANS**. There are five oceans:

the Arctic, Atlantic, Indian, Pacific, and Southern. Together, the oceans account for 71 percent of the earth's surface and 97 percent of the earth's water.

Oceans are subject to cyclic rising and falling water levels at shorelines called **TIDES**, which are the result of the gravitational pull of the moon and sun. The oceans also experience **WAVES**, which are caused by the movement of energy through the water.

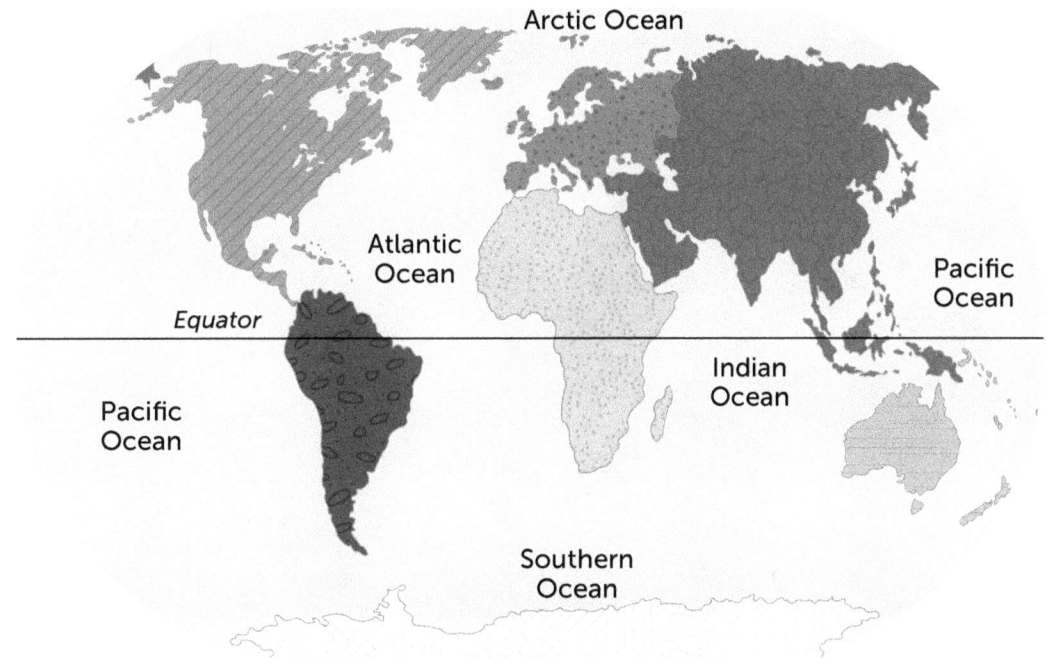

Figure 4.3. The Earth's Oceans

Other bodies of water include **LAKES**, which are usually freshwater, and **SEAS**, which are usually saltwater. **RIVERS** and streams are moving bodies of water that flow into lakes, seas, and oceans. The earth also contains groundwater, or water that is stored underground in rock formations called **AQUIFERS**.

Much of the earth's water is stored as **ICE**. The North and South Poles are usually covered in large sheets of ice called polar ice. **GLACIERS** are large masses of ice and snow that move. Over long periods of time, they scour Earth's surface, creating features such as lakes and valleys. Large chunks of ice that break off from glaciers are called **ICEBERGS**.

DID YOU KNOW?
97 percent of the water on earth is saltwater. 68 percent of the remaining freshwater is locked up in ice caps and glaciers.

The **WATER CYCLE** is the circulation of water throughout the earth's surface, atmosphere, and hydrosphere. Water on the earth's surface evaporates, or changes from a liquid to a gas, and becomes water vapor. Plants also release water vapor through transpiration. Water vapor in the air then comes together to form clouds. When it cools, this water vapor condenses into a liquid and falls from the sky as precipitation, which includes rain, sleet, snow, and hail. Precipitation replenishes groundwater and the water found in features such as lakes and rivers, thus starting the cycle over again.

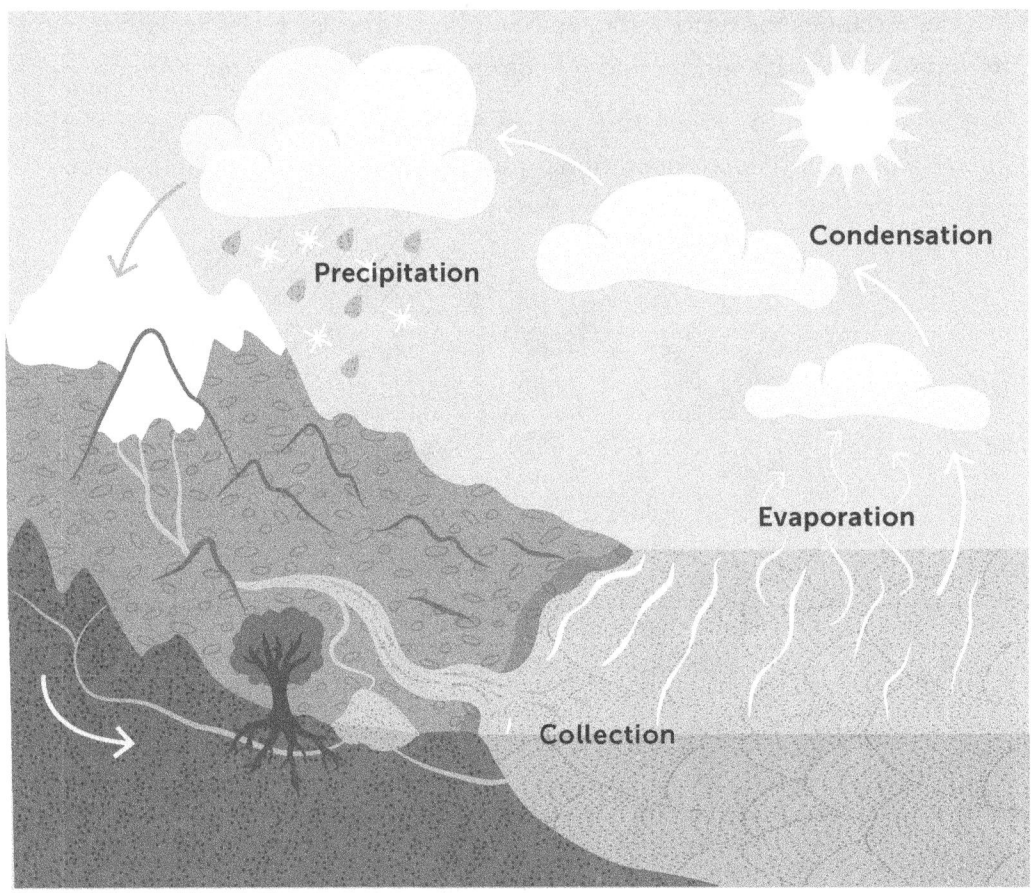

Figure 4.4. The Water Cycle

EXAMPLE

3. During the water cycle, groundwater is replenished by
   A) transpiration.
   B) glaciers.
   C) lakes.
   D) precipitation.

Meteorology

Above the surface of Earth is the mass of gases called the **ATMOSPHERE**. The atmosphere includes the **TROPOSPHERE**, which is closest to the earth, followed by the **STRATOSPHERE**, **MESOSPHERE**, and **THERMOSPHERE**. The outermost layer of the atmosphere is the **EXOSPHERE**, which is located 6,200 miles above the surface. Generally, temperature in the atmosphere decreases with altitude. The **OZONE LAYER**, which captures harmful radiation from the sun, is located in the stratosphere.

The **HUMIDITY**, or amount of water vapor in the air, and the **TEMPERATURE** are two major atmospheric conditions that determine weather, the day-to-day changes in atmospheric conditions. A **WARM FRONT** occurs when warm air moves over a cold air mass, causing the air to feel warmer and more humid. A **COLD FRONT** occurs when cold air moves under a warm air mass, causing a drop in temperature.

> **DID YOU KNOW?**
> Between each layer, a boundary exists where conditions change. This boundary takes the first part of the name of the previous layer followed by "pause." For example, the boundary between the troposphere and stratosphere is called the tropopause.

Sometimes, weather turns violent. Tropical cyclones, or hurricanes, originate over warm ocean water. Hurricanes have destructive winds of more than 74 miles per hour and create large storm surges that can cause extensive damage along coastlines. Hurricanes, typhoons, and cyclones are all the same type of storm; they just have different names based on where the storm is located. **HURRICANES** originate in the Atlantic or Eastern Pacific Ocean, **TYPHOONS** in the Western Pacific Ocean, and **CYCLONES** in the Indian Ocean. **TORNADOES** occur when unstable warm and cold air masses collide and a rotation is created by fast-moving winds.

The long-term weather conditions in a geographic location are called **CLIMATE**. A climate zone is a large area that experiences similar average temperature and precipitation. The three major climate zones, based on temperature, are the polar, temperate, and tropical zones. Each climate zone is subdivided into subclimates that have unique characteristics. The **TROPICAL CLIMATE ZONE** (warm temperatures) can be subdivided into tropical wet, tropical wet and dry, semiarid, and arid. The **TEMPERATE CLIMATE ZONES** (moderate temperatures) include Mediterranean, humid subtropical, marine West Coast, humid continental, and subarctic. The **POLAR CLIMATE ZONES** (cold temperatures) include tundra, highlands, nonpermanent ice, and ice cap. Polar climates are cold and experience prolonged, dark winters due to the tilt of the earth's axis.

EXAMPLE

4. Which layer of the atmosphere absorbs harmful ultraviolet radiation from the sun?
   - **A)** mesosphere
   - **B)** stratosphere
   - **C)** troposphere
   - **D)** thermosphere

Test Your Knowledge

Read the question, and then choose the most correct answer.

1. Which planet orbits closest to Earth?
   A) Mercury
   B) Venus
   C) Jupiter
   D) Saturn

2. What is the name of the phenomenon when a star suddenly increases in brightness and then disappears from view?
   A) aurora
   B) black hole
   C) eclipse
   D) supernova

3. How long does it take the earth to rotate on its axis?
   A) one hour
   B) one day
   C) one month
   D) one year

4. Which statement about the solar system is true?
   A) Earth is much closer to the sun than it is to other stars.
   B) The moon is closer to Venus than it is to Earth.
   C) At certain times of the year, Jupiter is closer to the sun than Earth is.
   D) Mercury is the closest planet to Earth.

5. When Earth moves between the moon and the sun, it is called a
   A) solar eclipse.
   B) lunar eclipse.
   C) black hole.
   D) supernova.

6. Which planet does not have a moon?
   A) Mercury
   B) Earth
   C) Jupiter
   D) Saturn

7. What is the term for the top layer of the earth's surface?
   A) lithosphere
   B) atmosphere
   C) biosphere
   D) asthenosphere

8. Which action is an example of mechanical weathering?
   A) Calcium carbonate reacts with water to form a cave.
   B) An iron gate rusts.
   C) Tree roots grow under the foundation of a house and cause cracks.
   D) Feldspar turns to clay when exposed to water.

9. Which of the following is caused by geothermal heat?
   A) geysers
   B) tsunamis
   C) tornadoes
   D) hurricanes

10. Which of the following holds the largest percentage of earth's freshwater?
    A) glaciers and ice caps
    B) groundwater
    C) lakes
    D) oceans

11. Which of the following best describes how igneous rocks are formed?
    A) Sediment is compacted by pressure in the earth to form rock.
    B) Magma comes to the earth's surface and cools to form rock.
    C) Chemical weathering changes the composition of a rock to form new rock.
    D) Ancient plant and animal life is calcified to create rock.

12. Which of the following is true as altitude increases in the troposphere?
    A) Temperature and pressure increase.
    B) Temperature increases and pressure decreases.
    C) Temperature and pressure decrease.
    D) Temperature decreases and pressure increases.

13. Which statement about hurricanes and tornadoes is true?
    A) Hurricanes and tornadoes spin in opposite directions.
    B) Tornadoes do not occur in warm climates.
    C) Tornadoes have a low wind velocity.
    D) Hurricanes are formed over warm ocean water.

14. Which two properties are used to classify climate zones?
    A) latitude and temperature
    B) temperature and precipitation
    C) elevation and latitude
    D) precipitation and tilt of Earth's axis

15. Which of the following best describes continental drift?
    A) The mass extinction of the earth's species that occurred when a meteor struck the earth.
    B) The spinning of the earth's inner core that creates the earth's magnetic field.
    C) The formation of land masses from cooled magma.
    D) The movement of tectonic plates in the lithosphere.

Earth and Space Science

Answer Key
EXAMPLES

1. **D) is correct.** When the moon moves between the earth and the sun, a solar eclipse occurs, blocking sunlight from the planet.

2. **A) is correct.** Igneous rocks form when liquid rock cools and solidifies.

3. **D) is correct.** Precipitation such as rain and snow seep into the ground to add to the groundwater supply.

4. **B) is correct.** The stratosphere contains a sublayer called the ozone layer, which absorbs harmful ultraviolet radiation from the sun.

TEST YOUR KNOWLEDGE

1. **B) is correct.** Venus's orbit is closest to Earth and is the second planet from the sun.

2. **D) is correct.** Before a star collapses, the star burns brighter for a period of time and then fades from view. This is a supernova.

3. **B) is correct.** Earth takes approximately twenty-four hours to rotate on its axis.

4. **A) is correct.** The sun is about ninety-three million miles from Earth; the next closest star is about twenty-five trillion miles away.

5. **B) is correct.** A lunar eclipse is when Earth moves between the moon and the sun.

6. **A) is correct.** Only the first two planets, Mercury and Venus, lack moons.

7. **A) is correct.** The lithosphere is the top layer of the earth's surface.

8. **C) is correct.** Mechanical weathering involves breaking a substance down without changing the composition of the substance.

9. **A) is correct.** Geysers are caused by geothermal heating of water underground.

10. **A) is correct.** Glaciers and ice caps contain approximately 68.7% of all of Earth's freshwater supply, which is the largest percentage of the resources listed.

11. **B) is correct.** Igneous rock is formed when magma (melted rock) is brought to the earth's surface and cools.

12. **C) is correct.** Temperature and pressure both decrease with altitude in the troposphere.

13. **D) is correct.** Hurricanes require warm ocean water to form.

14. **B) is correct.** Climate zones are classified by temperature and precipitation.

15. **D) is correct.** Continental drift is the movement of tectonic plates that lead to the current position of the continents.

Follow the link below for your second Science GED practice test:
www.acceptedinc.com/ged-2018-online-resources

CHAPTER FIVE
Practice Test

Multiple Choice
Read the passage and/or question, and then choose the most correct answer.

1. A chemical reaction occurs when one or more reactants undergoes a chemical change to produce new substances called products. The reaction is described in a chemical equation with the reactants on the left, the products on the right, and an arrow in the middle. Five types of chemical reactions are shown in the following table.

Type of Reaction	General Formula
Synthesis	A + B → C
Decomposition	A → B + C
Single displacement	AB + C → A + BC
Double displacement	AB + CD → AC + BD
Combustion	$C_xH_yO_z + O_2 → CO_2 + H_2O$

   Based on the information in the table, which of the following is a decomposition reaction?
   A) $2Na + Cl_2 → 2NaCl$
   B) $Zn + 2HCl → ZnCl_2 + H_2$
   C) $CH_4 + 2O_2 → CO_2 + 2H_2O$
   D) $H_2CO_3 → H_2O + CO_2$

2. Water moves across cell membranes through the process of osmosis. The concentration of solute inside and outside a cell will determine which way water moves across the membrane. Water molecules will move down their concentration gradient, meaning they will move from areas of high concentration to areas of low concentration. In other words, water will flow into the cell when the solute concentration in the cell is higher than the environment. The reverse is also true—water will flow out of the cell when the solute concentration is lower in the cell than in the surrounding environment.

   A certain prokaryotic organism typically lives in a 10 percent saline concentration environment. Which of the following environments would cause the organism to lose mass due to osmosis?

   A) a solution of pure water
   B) a solution of 5 percent saline concentration
   C) a solution of 10 percent saline concentration
   D) a solution of 20 percent saline concentration

3. Electrical charge can be positive (+), negative (−), or neutral. Objects that are both positive or both negative will repel each other. Objects that have opposing positive and negative charges will be attracted to each other. Neutral objects will not be affected by either positive or negative objects.

   Two negative charges are held at a distance of 1 meter from each other. What will the charges do when they are released?

   A) remain at rest
   B) move closer together
   C) move farther apart
   D) move together in the same direction

4. A phylogenetic tree is a diagram that shows the evolutionary relationship between species based on their genetic and phenotypic similarities. Each node, where a branch starts, represents the most recent common ancestor shared by the species on the branches extending from that node.

   On the diagram, select the node(s) that represent common ancestors shared by species H and K.

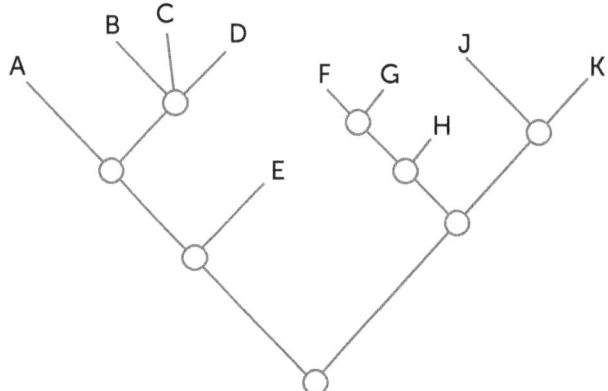

Use the following passage to answer questions 5 and 6.

A scientist designs an experiment to test the hypothesis that exposure to more sunlight will increase the growth rate of elodea, a type of aquatic plant. The scientist has accumulated data from previous experiments that identify the average growth rate of elodea exposed to natural sunlight in the wild.

In the experiment setup, there are three tanks housing ten elodea each. Tank A is positioned in front of a window to receive natural sunlight similar to what elodea are exposed to; tank B is positioned in front of the same window but has an additional sunlight-replicating lamp affixed to it; and tank C is positioned in a dark corner with no exposure to natural sunlight.

5. When setting up the preceding experiment, the scientist has the option of using a separate water filter for each of the three tanks or using a single filtration system that attaches all three and affects them simultaneously. Which of the following filter setups makes a more valid experiment and why?
    A) separate filters for each of the three tanks, because this ensures a higher quality of water for each tank
    B) one filtration system for all three tanks, because this makes filtration a controlled variable
    C) one filtration system for all three tanks, because this reduces the workload for the researcher
    D) separate filters for each of the three tanks, because this adds another variable to be tested and analyzed for inclusion in the experiment's results

6. Which of the following is the control group in the preceding experiment?
    A) tank A
    B) tank B
    C) tank C
    D) There is no control group in this experiment.

7. Weathering is the breaking down of rocks, minerals, and organic materials. Weathering can be either mechanical or chemical. Mechanical weathering occurs when a material is physically torn apart. Chemical weathering occurs when a chemical reaction causes the material to decompose, forming new materials in the process.

    Which action is an example of mechanical weathering?
    A) Calcium carbonate reacts with water to form a cave.
    B) An iron gate rusts.
    C) Tree roots grow under the foundation of a house and cause cracks.
    D) Bananas turn brown after they are peeled.

Use the following passage and figure to answer questions 8 and 9.

Gastric lipase is an enzyme that breaks down fat produced by cells that line the stomach. α-amylase is an enzyme produced in the pancreas that helps break down starches into simple sugars. It is released into the small intestine.

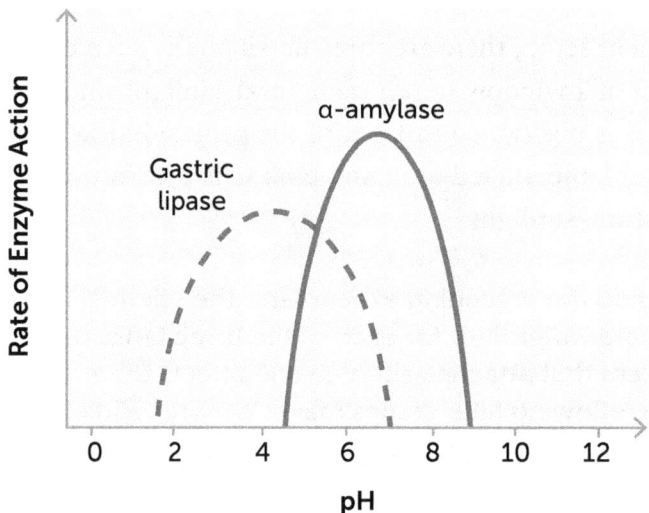

8. The small intestine has a pH higher than 7. According to the graph, what will happen to the activity of gastric lipase when it enters the small intestine?

    A) Its activity will increase.
    B) Its activity will remain the same.
    C) Its activity will increase initially, then decrease.
    D) Its activity will decrease.

9. According to the preceding graph, what is the optimal pH level for α-amylase?

    A) 4
    B) 6
    C) 7
    D) 9

10. Activation energy is the energy required for a chemical reaction to occur. If the activation energy for a reaction is too high, a reaction may not proceed or may proceed only at a very slow rate. The activation energy can be modified by the addition of a catalyst. A catalyst is a compound that lowers the activation energy of a reaction by changing the mechanism of the reaction to one with a lower activation energy. This process will increase the rate of the chemical reaction.

    A catalyst increases a reaction rate by doing which of the following?

    A) increasing the activation energy
    B) increasing the concentration of the reactants
    C) changing the type of energy required to move the reaction forward
    D) changing the reaction mechanism

Use the following graph to answer questions 11 and 12.

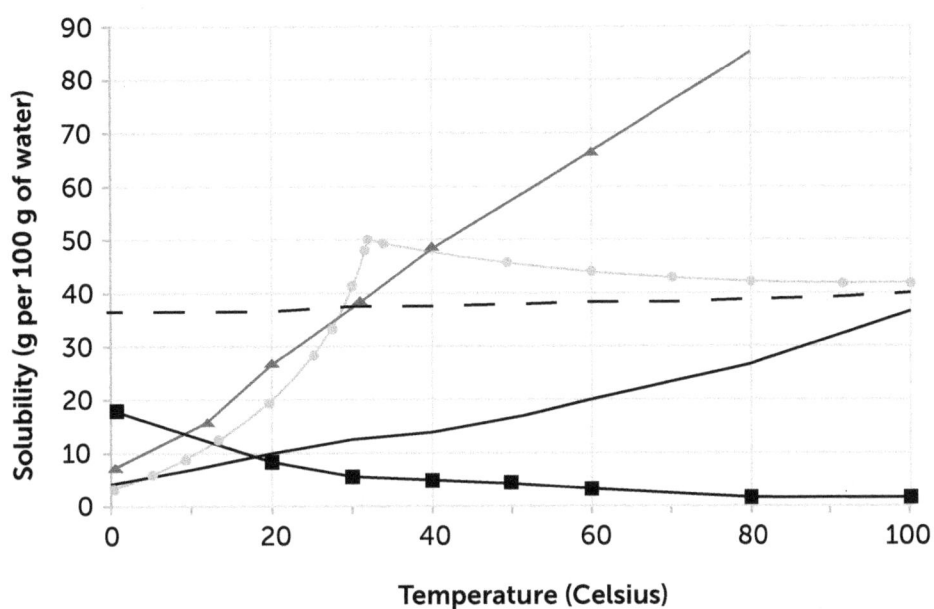

11. Which of the salts on the preceding solubility curve graph has the greatest solubility at 50°C?
    A) Na_2SO_4
    B) NaCl
    C) $Ba(NO_3)_2$
    D) Na_2HAsO_4

12. At what temperature is the highest mass of NaCl soluble in 100 grams of water?
    A) 0°C
    B) 40°C
    C) 80°C
    D) 100°C

13. As a gas giant, the planet Jupiter has a much lower density than terrestrial planets. Earth has a density of 5.51 grams per cubic centimeter, but Jupiter's density is only 1.33 grams per cubic centimeter. The largest planet in the solar system, Jupiter has a radius of 71,492 kilometers, a remarkable size more than ten times that of Earth. By volume, more than 1,300 Earths would fit within Jupiter. Jupiter has a solid core and a gaseous atmosphere that transitions slowly into a liquid state with no definable lower boundary.

Which of the following planets is most similar to Jupiter?

	Planet	Density (grams per cm³)	Radius (miles)
A)	Neptune	1.6	24,746
B)	Mercury	5.4	1,516
C)	Mars	3.9	3,396
D)	Venus	5.2	6,051

14. An experiment was conducted to study the effect of temperature on the survival rate of a fish species. The study included five populations, each held for ten days at a different temperature. The number of individuals in each population was recorded after five days and after ten days. The results are shown in the following table.

Temperature	Survival Rate		
	Day 1	Day 5	Day 10
15°C	100%	94%	80%
20°C	100%	96%	94%
25°C	100%	84%	73%
30°C	100%	81%	58%
35°C	100%	72%	41%

Which of the following statements is supported by the observations recorded in the table?

A) The population held at 30°C had the lowest survival rate after ten days.

B) Of the five populations, only the one held at 35°C had a survival rate of less than 50 percent after ten days.

C) After ten days, the survival rate of the population held at 30°C was half the survival rate of the population held at 15°C.

D) The survival rate after five days was lowest for the population held at 30°C.

15. A scientist discovers a new species of snail that lives in the ocean. He tested the ability of this species to handle heat by measuring its growth rate as he increased the temperature of the water. He also tested two different concentrations of salt to determine which type of marine environment the snail would be best suited for.

Which of the following is the dependent variable in the experiments described above?

A) salt concentration
B) temperature
C) growth rate
D) number of snails

16. Each cell organelle performs a specific task within a cell. The genetic material, which contains the code needed to produce proteins, is held in the nucleus. Ribosomes produce proteins that are processed and transported by the Golgi apparatus. In plant cells, chloroplasts transform the sun's energy into sugar; in both plants and animals, mitochondria transform sugar into the energy-rich molecule ATP. Waste products from all these processes are stored in vacuoles.

Which of the following cells would likely contain a higher than normal number of mitochondria?

A) muscle cell
B) skin cell
C) egg
D) red blood cell

17. A system is the part of the universe where an actual process takes place or where observations are made; the rest of the universe is the surroundings. There are three types of systems. An open system allows the exchange of energy or matter between the system and its surrounding. In a closed system, only exchange of energy between the system and its surroundings is possible; exchange of matter is not possible. Finally, in an isolated system there is no exchange of energy or matter between the system and its surroundings.

Which of the following is a closed system?

A) a glass of water at room temperature
B) a balloon filled with warm water
C) an insulated container filled with ice water
D) an uncovered pot of boiling water on the stove

18. A survivorship curve shows the percentage of individuals in a population who survive over time. Type I species produce a small number of offspring and care closely for them. Type III species produce large numbers of offspring but do little or no caretaking for their young. Type II species show a balance between number of offspring and caretaking.

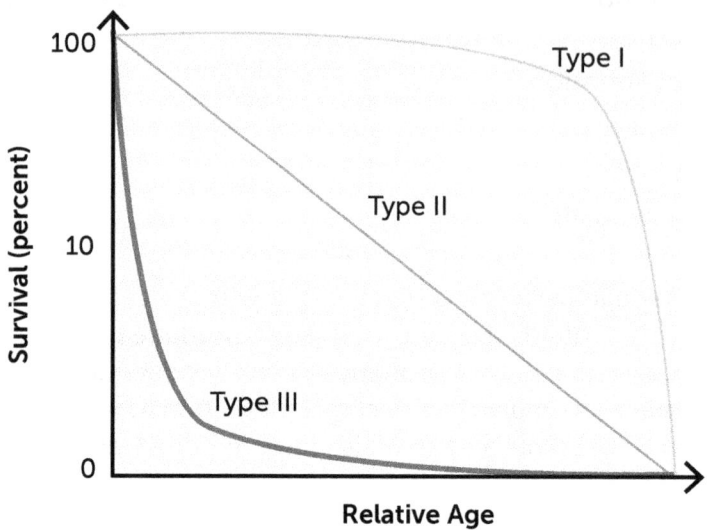

Which survivorship curve would describe each of the species in the following table? Write your answer in the space provided.

Species	Survivorship Curve
mice	
humans	
oak trees	
ducks	

Use the following table to answer questions 19 and 20.

Planet	Mass	Acceleration Due to Gravity (g)
Mercury	3.18×10^{23}	3.59
Earth	5.98×10^{24}	9.81
Mars	6.42×10^{23}	3.77
Jupiter	1.90×10^{27}	25.95
Neptune	1.03×10^{26}	14.07

19. Free fall is a type of motion in which the only force acting on an object is gravity. The velocity of an object in free fall is described the equation $v = gt$, where v is velocity, g is the acceleration due to gravity, and t is time.

On which planet would an object reach the highest speed after being in free fall for three seconds?

- **A)** Earth
- **B)** Mars
- **C)** Jupiter
- **D)** Neptune

20. Weight (W) is defined as the force exerted on an object by gravity. It is equal to the acceleration due to gravity (g) times the object's mass (m): $W = ga$.

On Earth, objects A and B have the same mass and weight. If object B is moved to Mars, which of the following statements is true?

- **A)** Object A now has a greater mass and weight.
- **B)** Object B now has a greater mass and weight.
- **C)** Both objects have the same mass, but object A now has the greater weight.
- **D)** Both objects have the same mass, but object B now has the greater weight.

Use the following passage to answer questions 21 and 22.

In a chemical reaction, it is only the number of electrons in an atom that changes—the nucleus remains unaffected. Conversely, in a nuclear reaction, changes occur in an atom's nucleus, affecting the number of protons, neutrons, or both. In a nuclear reaction, unstable atoms called radioisotopes spontaneously emit particles and energy.

The time it takes for substances to decay varies widely—some radioisotopes decay completely in only a few seconds, whereas others decay over millions of years. The time it takes for half of a sample to decay is that substance's half-life (h or $t^{\frac{1}{2}}$). The equation for half-life is written as

$$A = A_0 \left(\frac{1}{2}\right)^{\left(\frac{t}{h}\right)}$$

where A is the final amount, A_0 is the initial amount, t is the time, and h is the half-life.

21. Which of the following is the best description of radioactive decay?

- **A)** the absorption of energy by an atom's nucleus
- **B)** the movement of electrons into an atom's nucleus
- **C)** the release of particles by the atom's nucleus
- **D)** the sharing of electrons between atoms

22. The half-life of iodine-131 is eight days. How much of a 120-gram sample of iodine-131 will remain after twenty-four days?

   A) 0 grams
   B) 15 grams
   C) 30 grams
   D) 60 grams

23. A team of ecologists tested the effect of parenting in a species of bird for a period of five years. For this particular bird species, both males and females cared for the young. During their research, the ecologists transferred chicks between sites to manufacture small broods of chicks (three to four), normal broods (five to six), and large broods (seven to eight). The researchers then measured the percentage of male and female parent birds that survived the winter. The data is represented in the graph.

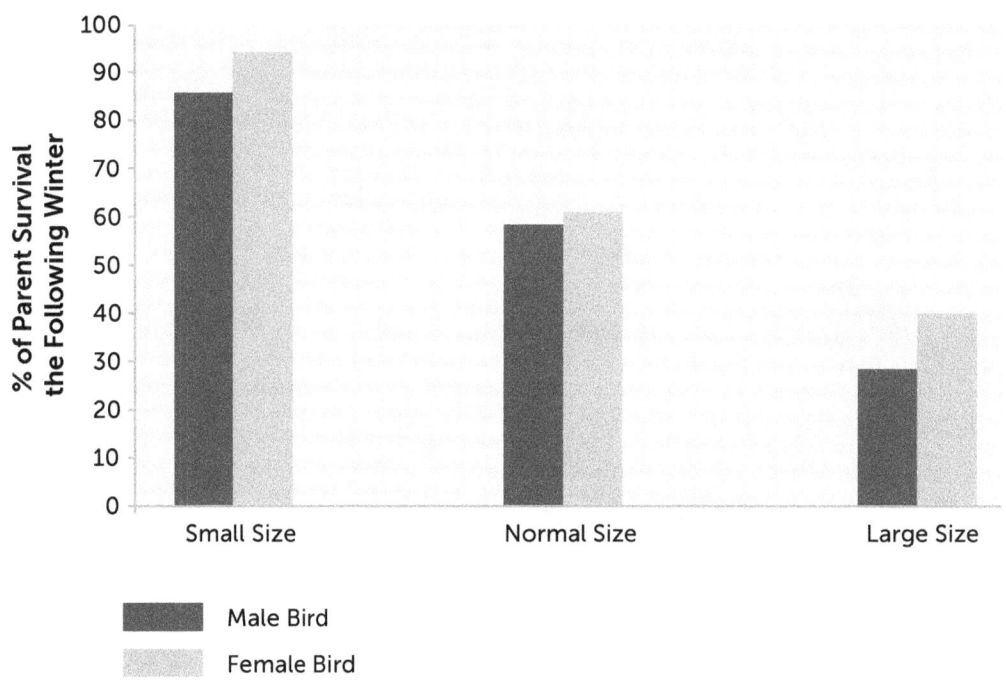

Which of the following conclusions would be accurate based on the data represented in the preceding graph?

   A) There is an apparent negative correlation between brood (nesting) size and parental survival.
   B) The chicks in the smaller nests received more food than those in the larger nest sites. This allowed them more weight gain and a better chance of surviving the winter.
   C) The survival rate of the female birds is more drastically affected by the larger nest sizes than the male birds.
   D) The survival rate of the male birds increased by 50 percent at the larger nest sizes than the smaller nest sizes.

24. In 1897, J.J. Thomson discovered the existence of electrons. Thomson incorporated the electron into a new model of the atom. He proposed that the atom had a spherical shape with a uniformly distributed positive charge. The electrons, which made up only a small portion of the atom's mass, were uniformly embedded in the positive mass. This model is also called the plum pudding model.

Ernest Rutherford built on Thomson's model of the atom by introducing the concept of the nucleus. From his experiments, Rutherford concluded that an atom is not just empty space with electrons distributed inside it. Instead, an atom has a positively charged nucleus that contains most of its mass.

Which of the following changes did Ernest Rutherford make to the plum pudding model of the atom?

- **A)** Rutherford claimed that an atom was composed of both positively and negatively charged particles.
- **B)** Rutherford claimed that the positive charge of the atom was contained in a small area at the center of the atom.
- **C)** Rutherford claimed that the nucleus of an atom contained both positive and neutral particles.
- **D)** Rutherford claimed that the mass of an atom was contained mostly in the electrons.

25. Three types of plate boundaries occur where tectonic plates meet. At a convergent plate boundary two tectonic plates move toward each other and collide, forming a mountain or a deep sea trench. At a divergent plate boundary, also called a spreading center or rift zone, the two plates are moving apart. This process creates rifts or valleys. At a transform plate boundary, the two plates are sliding past each other, causing a great deal of friction and a large buildup of energy that may be released in the form of an earthquake.

Which type of plate boundary is shown in the following diagram?

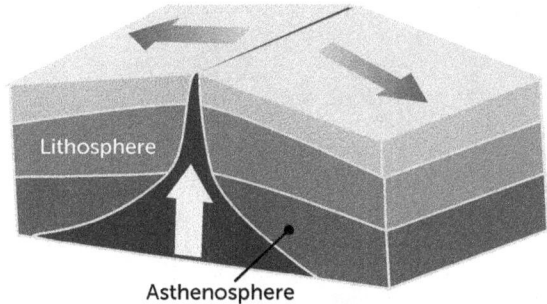

- **A)** convergent plate boundary
- **B)** divergent plate boundary
- **C)** transform plate boundary

26. The volume and temperature of a gas are directly proportional. When temperature is increased and pressure is held constant, the volume of the gas will expand. This relationship is described in Charles's law:

$$\frac{V_1}{T_1} = \frac{V_2}{T_2}$$

where V_1 is the gas's initial volume, V_2 is final volume, T_1 is initial temperature, and T_2 is final temperature.

A balloon is filled with 1 liter of helium. If the temperature of the air inside the balloon goes down, what will happen to the balloon?

A) The volume of the helium will increase, and the balloon will expand.

B) The volume of the helium will decrease, and the balloon will shrink.

C) The volume of the helium will not change, and the balloon will stay the same size.

Use the following passage and the diagram to answer questions 27 and 28.

The circulatory system includes two closed loops. In the pulmonary loop, deoxygenated blood leaves the heart and travels to the lungs, where it loses carbon dioxide and becomes rich in oxygen. The oxygenated blood then returns to the heart, which pumps it through the systemic loop. The systemic loop delivers oxygen to the rest of the body and returns deoxygenated blood to the heart.

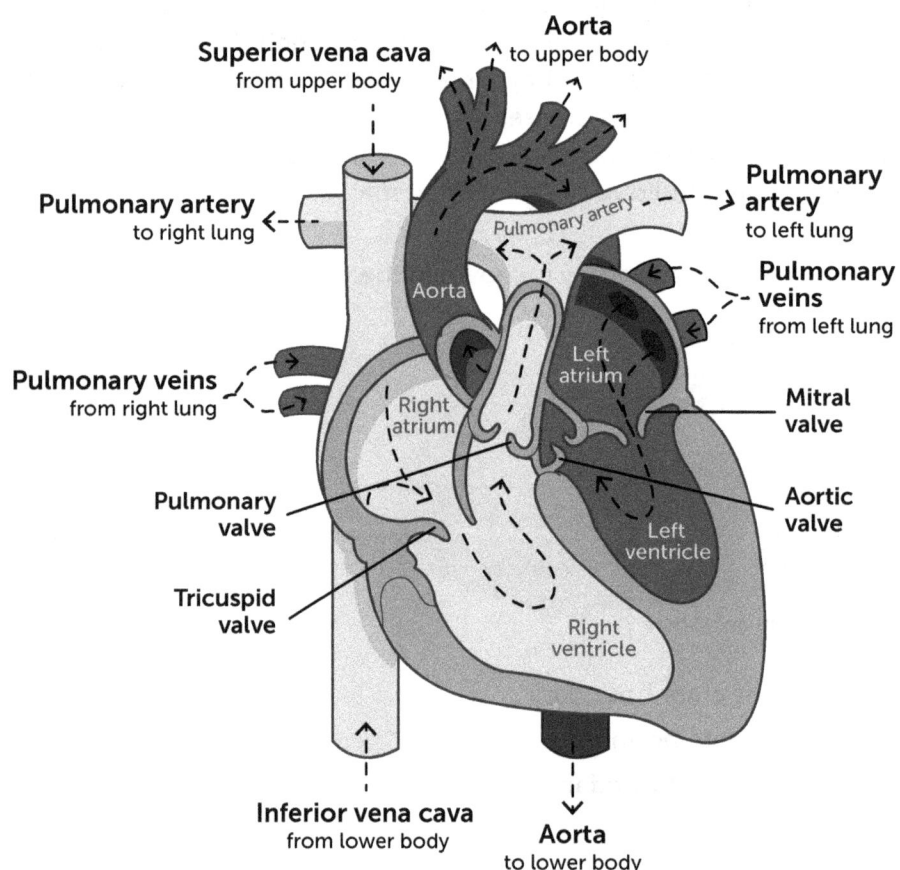

27. Select the blood vessel(s) that carry oxygenated blood.
- ☐ aorta
- ☐ superior vena cava
- ☐ inferior vena cava
- ☐ pulmonary artery
- ☐ pulmonary veins

28. Place the four chambers of the heart to show the path followed by blood through the heart.

left ventricleright ventricle

left atriumright atrium

lungs → _____ → _____ → _____ → _____ → body

29. Entropy is often described as a measure of randomness or chaos in a system. It can also be thought of as the number of possible configurations, or microstates, within a system. Increasing the number of possible microstates in a system will increase the chaos or randomness of a system: with increasing possible configurations, it is less likely that molecules will be in a particular microstate. This principle explains why gases spontaneously expand: molecules have more possible arrangements when they have more space to move around.

Systems will favor processes that create more possible configurations for the molecules in the system. Entropy will increase when temperature, volume, or the number of molecules in the system increases.

Which of the following changes will increase the entropy of the system?

A) splitting water to form hydrogen gas and oxygen gas

B) freezing gaseous carbon dioxide to form dry ice

C) using a piston to compress the air in a cylinder

D) condensing water from the atmosphere on a cold glass surface

30. Use the periodic table on page 39 to answer the following question.

The molar mass of a compound is found by adding the molar mass of the individual atoms that make up the molecule. What is the molar mass of hydrogen peroxide (H_2O_2)? Write your answer in grams per mole in the box below.

Answer Key

1. **D) is correct.** This is a decomposition reaction in which a single reactant produces two products.

2. **D) is correct.** Increasing the solution to 20 percent solute concentration would cause water to flow out of the cell, causing its mass to decrease.

3. **C) is correct.** Objects with the same charge will repel each other, so two negative charges will move farther apart.

4.

[phylogenetic tree diagram with species A, B, C, D, E, F, G, H, J, K and two marked ancestor nodes]

The two marked nodes are common ancestors shared by species H and K. The branch containing species H diverges from the branch containing species K at the second node.

5. **B) is correct.** Using one filtration system for all three tanks keeps the water quality across all three tanks constant and eliminates experimental bias for this variable.

6. **A) is correct.** Tank A is the control group because the sunlight variable is unchanged from the sunlight the elodea are exposed to in their natural environment.

7. **C) is correct.** The tree root is breaking up the rocks and minerals that form the foundation of the house without changing their chemical composition. The other choices are examples of chemical weathering.

8. **D) is correct.** From the graph, it is clear that the activity of gastric protease drops off completely at a pH around 7. Entering the small intestine with a pH greater than 7 would cause the enzyme reactivity to decrease or stop completely.

9. **C) is correct.** The highest point on the graph for α-amylase is its optimal pH level because that is where it is the most reactive. According to this graph, that level is a pH of 7.

10. **D) is correct.** A catalyst reduces the activation energy by creating an alternative reaction mechanism for the reaction.

11. **D) is correct.** The solubility for Na_2HAsO_4 at 50°C is around 55 grams per 100 grams of water. This is the highest for the solutes listed on the graph.

12. **D) is correct.** At 100°C about 40 grams of NaCl is soluble. The solubility of NaCl decreases with a decrease in temperature.

13. **A) is correct.** Neptune, like Jupiter, has a low density and a large radius.

14. **B) is correct.** At day 10, the population held at 35°C had a survival rate of 41 percent, which is less than 50 percent. All the

other populations have a survival rate greater than 50 percent.

15. **C) is correct.** The growth rate is the variable that is dependent on the changes to water temperature and concentration of salt in the water.

16. **A) is correct.** Muscle cells use ATP to create muscle contractions, so they need high numbers of mitochondria to produce the needed ATP.

17. **B) is correct.** A closed system allows exchange of energy but not matter with its surroundings. Matter (water) cannot enter or leave the balloon, but energy in the form of heat can penetrate the balloon. Choices A and D are open systems, and choice C is an isolated system.

18.

Species	Survivorship Curve
mice	**Type III**
humans	**Type I**
oak trees	**Type III**
ducks	**Type II**

19. **C) is correct.** The acceleration due to gravity is highest on Jupiter, so the object's speed would increase at the greatest rate on Jupiter.

20. **C) is correct.** The mass of an object is constant. The weight of an object depends on the force of gravity that the object experiences. The gravity on the surface of Mars is less than Earth's, so object B will have the same mass but a smaller weight.

21. **C) is correct.** During radioactive decay, an atom's nucleus emits particles and energy, which changes the composition of the atom's nucleus.

22. **B) is correct.** Use the half-life equation:

$$A = A_0 \left(\frac{1}{2}\right)^{\left(\frac{t}{h}\right)} = (120 \text{ g})\left(\frac{1}{2}\right)^{\left(\frac{24}{8}\right)} = (120 \text{ g})\left(\frac{1}{2}\right)^3 = (120 \text{ g})\left(\frac{1}{8}\right) = \mathbf{15 \text{ g}}$$

23. **A) is correct.** From the data on the graph, there is a clear correlation between increased size of bird nest and parent mortality.

24. **B) is correct.** Ernest Rutherford introduced the concept of the nucleus, which he claimed contained the positive charge of the atom and most of its mass.

25. **B) is correct.** At a divergent plate boundary, the plates are moving away from each other forming a trench or valley.

26. **B) is correct.** The volume of the balloon will decrease when the temperature of the gas inside is decreased. This can be shown by plugging values into the formula for Charles's law (the exact numbers don't matter).

27. ☑ aorta
    ☐ superior vena cava
    ☐ inferior vena cava
    ☐ pulmonary artery
    ☑ pulmonary veins

The aorta carries oxygenated blood to the body, and the pulmonary veins carry oxygenated blood from the lungs to the heart.

28. lungs → right atrium → right ventricle → left atrium → left ventricle → body

29. **A) is correct.** Splitting a single water molecule to form two molecules ($H_2O \rightarrow H_2 + O_2$) increases the number of molecules in the system, increasing entropy. The other choices decrease entropy by decreasing temperature or volume.

30. The molar mass of H_2O_2 is 2(1 g) + 2(16 g) = **34 grams per mole**.

www.ingramcontent.com/pod-product-compliance
Lightning Source LLC
Chambersburg PA
CBHW081925170426
43200CB00014B/2832